# AN UNSCHOOLER'S GUIDE:

## How to Quit School And Go To College

Merridith Curry

# An Unschooler's Guide:

## How To Quit School And Go To College

ISBN 978-0-9855438-0-8

Published by

Merridith Curry

Edited by

Norma Curry

Cover artwork by Merridith Curry

P.O. Box 62459

Cincinnati, Ohio 45241

To my mom,

For being my teacher, my coach, my support and guide. Without you this book would never have been written. Thank you for all your love and all your wisdom.

I love you.



And to the following strong women who inspired, supported, and mentored me:

Ruth Anne Wolfe and Regina Hall

# Contents

# Introduction

*"It is, in fact, nothing short of a miracle that the modern methods of instruction have not yet entirely strangled the holy curiosity of inquiry; for this delicate little plant, aside from stimulation, stands mainly in need of freedom; without this it goes to wreck and ruin without fail. It is a very grave mistake to think that the enjoyment of seeing and searching can be promoted by means of coercion and a sense of duty. To the contrary, I believe it would be possible to rob even a healthy beast of prey of its voraciousness, if it were possible, with the aid of a whip, to force the beast to devour continuously, even when not hungry, especially if the food, handed out under such coercion, were to be selected accordingly."-Albert Einstein*

Imagine waking up in the morning and not rushing to catch the school bus, not ushering the children out the door, not worrying about homework assignments, backpacks, selecting coats and hats, packing healthy lunches. Imagine a morning in which everyone rises not feeling grumpy or stressed, but instead excited to continue or start reading a book, to work on a project, to visit the zoo, the museum, to bake homemade cinnamon rolls, to hike in the park, or to participate in another favorite activity. How would you feel if you could begin every school day like this? How would starting each morning this way change your family, influence your way of living? Can you conceive of the benefits created from the laughter, the play and growth fostered through self-directed learning, otherwise known as unschooling? Would you believe that children who unschool look forward to mornings like this every single day of the year?

For those unfamiliar with home education, unschooling must sound like a strange term. However, in the realm of home education, unschooling is simply an alternative, one option that a family might choose. Unconventional and uncommon, those who select unschooling tend to recognize that some people attach a negative stigma to this idea. When first mentioning unschooling I frequently encounter confused stares and those who ask, "Unschooling? What's that?"

After years of explaining to coworkers and acquaintances, I more often than not simply refer to myself as home educated. Not that I'm embarrassed by my educational choice, but I'd rather not explain unschooling to someone I've just met, which often equates to trying to explain to a fish how I ride a bicycle. Neither the fish nor the bicycle rider can understand each other, both coming from completely different perspectives. Unschooling extends way beyond the limited perspective found in the preset, controlled curricular boundaries of most institutional learning. By comparison, unschooling stretches out like an endless ocean, filling every perceivable angle with vast possibilities. Today the full depths of unschooling, like the ocean, await exploration, whereas the boundaries and limitations of institutionalized learning have suffered meticulous research and dissection, yet remain much the same as they were when compulsory attendance became the law in this country.

What separates unschooling and other traditional educational approaches arises from fundamentally different psychological and philosophical perspectives, unschoolers easily recognize that individuals instinctively seek learning, without much guidance, instruction, poking or prodding. Like the instinct that prompts a baby bird to fly at the exact moment its instincts and biology meld, urging it to spread and flap its wings, learning is an integral part of human nature. No one teaches the bird to fly, nor does anyone teach the butterfly how to free itself from its cocoon. Even though the lives we elect to live and create far exceed the basic and instinctive survival skills of a bird or butterfly, the lessons remain the same. All life consists of complicated and challenging moments. How we survive those moments hinges more on instincts and not so much on prior instruction or experience. Inside all of us the natural fight or flight response will ordinarily override any other impetus.

Expecting a child to sit and read a textbook full of facts that educators have deemed worthy of his or her learning is like sitting a lion, a complete carnivore, before a bowl of vegetables, expecting the lion to eat the vegetables. Neither child nor lion will readily consume something just because it's right there. Do the facts in the textbook relate to anything in the child's life? Has the child expressed a desire to study those facts? Does the lion desire vegetables? No. Both scenarios defy nature.

When you open a child to opportunities, learning occurs through enjoyable activity and the child will learn. Similarly, if a lion wants to eat, it can only depend on its mother or watching other lions hunt for so long before it tries to hunt for itself. If a child longs to fly a kite or ride a bike, he or she will best grasp the principles of these activities through hands-on involvement, not by listening to someone explain how to hold the string or grip the handlebars. You can spread an assortment of books on a table for a child, but that doesn't mean he or she will elect to read any of them. You can lead a horse to water, well, you know what I'm saying. When something grabs our attention we will often hold onto it with both hands: the strings of a balloon, the handlebars of a bicycle, the kite string, the first shoes we tie, the people we love. While every moment presents learning opportunities, situations that could teach us something, a student sitting in a chair at a desk, reading books or listening to a parent or teacher lecture, doesn't guarantee that learning will necessarily follow. If learning were so easy every child who regularly attends a public school would successfully pass his or her annual tests and go on to college in this one-size-fits-all idealistic approach to education. Why should parents or students accept that children must all learn the same way simply because someone else has decided that's how it should be?

The truth might surprise you. Turns out unschooling, or passion driven learning, began it all. Before school houses, before licensed and certified teachers in brick and mortar school buildings, children learned by doing. Parents taught their children the skills needed to survive, like how to find food, make clothes, cook, build a fire, erect a shelter. Throughout every culture children have learned by doing what comes naturally, by engaging in activities that contribute to his or her immediate and future well-being. Nowadays children accumulate a limited amount of knowledge that they might extend toward attaining more knowledge. They then might apply this knowledge to a job that a child might or might not seek as an adult. All information taught to children today stems from the concept of learning a specific set of rules, ideas and facts. These facts can vary greatly from state to state and school district to school district. Children living a mile apart from each other, but attending schools in two different school districts, experience completely different kinds of education. What they learn each day and the academic standards to which they are held will differ greatly, as well, from school to school as well as from state to state.

Over the course of 12 years in public schools, children across this country will all face assessment exams that may vary significantly in both rigor and subject matter covered, yet all college-bound children will need to take the same exams, either the ACT or SAT I, for admission at most colleges. During the majority of hours spent in school, publicly schooled children learn to pass tests, though not tests specifically geared to prepare them for college. Instead these assessments intend to somehow measure a child's academic growth from one year to the next. Measuring the intellectual growth of an individual should never rely solely on words written on an answer sheet, especially when every state has a different opinion of what a child should know by specific intellectual developmental stages.

If a child wants to attend college he or she can do so by simply preparing for and taking the ACT or SAT I exam and asking a parent to maintain a detailed transcript to accompany the student's admissions application to chosen colleges. Do the colleges ask for copies of these assessment tests? No. They look solely at composite scores, for each section and for the whole test. So why make students take assessments tests? Schools continue to maintain the importance of these tests as the gauge of who is and who isn't getting an education. In truth, the typical government mandated education usually demands a great deal less than what a home educated student could opt to study. After electing to exercise the right to educate one's children at home, a child can explore and investigate all kinds of educational activities, since no restrictions on time or resources limit this type of free-range curriculum. Going to visit the zoo, museums, historical sites, nature centers, plays, concerts, lectures, fairs, historical reenactments, state parks, wildlife reserves, factories, National Parks, and so much more, can fill a whole curriculum with field trips or weekly activities, instead of a few yearly events. The possibilities of what a child can learn far outreach those available for the typical government educated student.

My main purpose for writing this book arose after talking to other home schooling families. Often the parents expressed concerns and fears, frequently asking: how would their child learn?; what should each child learn?; would the parents know enough?; should the child be graded and tested?; how can parents encourage a child to write, or read, or learn math? I realized that parents ask themselves the same questions that parents might ask teachers when a child attends public schools. However home educating parents often discuss these questions with seasoned home schoolers who most often will reassure them by relaying stories of their own struggles and successes, telling tales of their journeys down that "road less taken." Realizing that one is not alone on this journey and that someone else knows and understands all those fears and concerns really motivated me to write a book about my own first-person unschooling experience. This isn't just someone's theory, an idea someone thinks sounds exciting and different, a case of wishful thinking or hopeful philosophy; I lived this. This book is the story of what I actually experienced. Like some sort of intangible and unreachable field of reality, home education can appear to be an enigma.

Perhaps the fact that the government system has conditioned parents to think that education can only succeed in a classroom with a state certified and licensed teacher and this has programmed parents to expect that something as vague, nebulous and ambiguous as unschooling could never succeed. However, children learn in a multitude of ways, many of which don't easily fit into an ordinary classroom situation. One teacher cannot accommodate the individual learning needs of every child, nor can each teacher replicate or support many common unschool type learning situations. But one parent, working independently with his or her child, can attempt to fulfill far more of those needs. Many parents tell me that they feel they are the best possible teachers for their children because no one knows their child's needs better. Surely the teacher in a crowded classroom cannot hope to know a child the way a mom or dad can. And in those families where parents and children talk to each other, share ideas and converse together, those evenings around the dinner table will often instigate new learning directions to explore, new insights to develop as well as a stronger, closer family.

Teachers might have the best intentions in mind when arriving in the public school classroom every weekday. Certainly one can find some stellar teachers in schools today. However, those stellar teachers do not tip the scales in favor of the public schools. When my mom began teaching English in the late 1960s she saw firsthand the problems in so many schools. She observed how teachers who barely passed the state's required teaching exams were allowed to instruct children. In one state where she taught, teachers only had to pass the teacher's exam with a composite score in the 13th percentile. That means those teachers only had to do better than the lowest scoring 13% of all those who had taken the exam. Yet these low-scoring teachers, who had all completed a college education as required by their state, could barely pass a pretty basic exam themselves. Many could not pass the essay writing section at all, though they could repeat that portion of the exam up to three times before the state would void their teaching credentials.

Not only are the standards that schools often apply to student testing dramatically dissimilar, so are those applied to the teachers entrusted to educate our children. I knew from the beginning that writing this book might upset some people. One of the many reasons why I procrastinated, stalling my completion of this book, was out of concern that I would face a great deal of backlash from those who are teachers and educators. After reviewing recent statistics on the bullying in public schools and talking with home educating families, I realized that I needed to write this book. I could no longer remain silent on the importance of having an alternative approach to learning available to those parents and students willing to take responsibility for their own and their family's learning.

When I talk to people about my education I spend a great deal of time explaining how I didn't have any issues with socializing, also known as the "S" word in home education circles, and that, yes, I did very well in college. I care so passionately about home education that I've walked away from money making opportunities because the people involved were so critical of home education. I won't deny that home education isn't always perfect, that it can be as flawed as any form of education. Believing that public education is right for every child and that every child can and should only learn the same way, in the same type of setting, however, ranks beyond flawed. Many parents have told me about some of their student's unexpected learning breakthrough moments, in all different places, all different situations. Sometimes those moments arose in grocery stores, in libraries, in the kitchen while cooking and measuring ingredients, or while sewing or knitting, making holiday gifts with other family members or friends.

Concerned parents need to realize that families from all backgrounds, living all over the world, and all over this country, successfully educate their children at home. Each day more families choose home education. If it truly caused as much harm as public education has caused, then home education would not be such a popular, growing trend. Instead many people are grasping that public schools just don't fulfill the educational needs of certain children, that these schools lack many important elements. My mom often mentions that when she taught English back in the 1960s many children were unable to read and write very well. Today that still remains a huge issue, perhaps bigger than it was in the nineteen-sixties. Colleges have been adding more remedial writing and math courses to their instruction due to the influx of freshmen who cannot pass required entry level college placement tests in these two subjects.

If public schools were succeeding and fulfilling their job, then wouldn't things have changed for the better since the 1960s when my mother was first teaching? Isn't it strange that with all the technology today, instead of students achieving higher and higher scores on required tests, yielding more capable and more highly skilled adults, we find students falling further behind, failing and dropping out of school in higher and higher percentages? What does that indicate about our legally mandated educational system? I think it indicates that we need to reconsider many of the fundamentals of education. Dedicated parents who spend entire days involved in activities to further the growth and interests of their children are fostering smart, independent thinkers through home education. These children learn the basics of reading, writing and mathematics early on, or whenever they are ready and motivated to learn these skills. Their parents, who spend every day fully engaged in the lives

16

of their children, understand exactly where that child stands academically. The parents see the books the student reads, look over the math worksheets, or engage in everyday math in the marketplace, ensuring that the child learns from his or her mistakes.

For the home educated student someone is almost always available when things get difficult. The doors to getting help don't close at the end of a preordained school day. When the parent is also the teacher, the teacher's on call 24/7. Home education changed my life. Everything about who I am today was the direct result of my alternative education. I might not fit into the cookie cutter mold of the average American young adult, but I challenge you to find anyone who does. I learned discipline and personal responsibility because of my self-directed learning. I taught myself the skills I needed to get into college and do well in college. I'm very proud of my accomplishments, proud of my education. Even though I didn't attend a school or take an assessment test after fourth grade, I still graduated from college. And I've held jobs since my teens, while enjoying a very active social life.

People rarely consider any other path than the one directly before them. Indeed, sometimes that path can be the best choice. However, for some an alternative path could prove more beneficial. In unschooling the family or child willing to explore can create a variety of alternative paths. Traditional schools set a more rigid route, restricting opportunity for expression and individual thought, whereas unschooling cultivates each individual child's creativity. It inspires the imagination, supports the dreamer and encourages personal growth.

You might look at the term unschooling and become instantly concerned about what it implies. How can a child learn anything while unschooling? I respond to that question by asking, how does a child learn anything while in a school? In school one spends so much time focused on "trivial pursuits," the memorization of facts, the shuffling from class to class, and the interruptions caused by other, often misbehaving, children.  Students at school spend less time than you think "getting an education".  Those instructional hours, often mandated by the state, can often be better spent outside the structured classroom.  Even though the unschooled student doesn't follow a set schedule every minute of the day, nor does he or she adhere to a strict curriculum everyday, self-directed learners are learning.  They may not be memorizing lots of facts and figures, but do these really matter?  Those facts and figures taught in school rarely, if ever, apply to practical adult living.  How many parents struggle as adults to help their children learn the same math they learned in grade school?

One should not assume that the unschooling parent needs to know everything about every subject their child needs or wants to learn.  But unschooling does require parents to practice patience and a willingness to learn with their child.  Besides, if a parent of an institutionally schooled child doesn't understand their child's homework, then how can that child get the support needed to learn?  Does the classroom teacher take the time to work with each individual student?  No, so that most of the time children who encounter difficulties simply don't learn.  Most schools relentlessly solicit volunteer tutors to work one-on-one with students.  If institutional schools require one-on-one instruction at school, in order for students to pass assessment exams, why even bother sending a child to school?  Unschooling children work together with each other, with older siblings and friends, and learn from and with their parents.  If a school needs tutors to assist them in teaching, tutors who frequently are not trained teachers themselves, then why can't a parent simply become the personal tutor for his or her own child?  Wouldn't you prefer to be the one teaching your child, rather than a stranger you haven't met, whose credentials, values and skills may be far less desirable than those of the parents?  Parents delude themselves when they expect that schools will always afford the best resources to teach children.

When I did attend a public school during my early elementary years the experience instilled in me a strong fear of failure. Though I only spent three years in public school (second, third and fourth grades), the feelings of never quite fulfilling some unseen educational requirement platform followed me until college. I thought that home education might have limited my ability to succeed at college and that I would find myself unprepared, but instead I discovered the opposite. In college I usually stood out as one of the most prepared and engaged students in all my classes. Finally, all those years of my mother telling me how smart I was, had proven her right.

People's opinions about home education can run the gamut. Some feel that home education adversely affects the child, while others can't stand the idea of having their children around all day, and some think that home educated students are just smarter than everyone else. Whatever your opinion might be, home education continues to grow in popularity every year. Fifteen to twenty years ago the majority of families who home educated did so for religious reasons. Now a wide range of families elect home education. My family chose home education for a number of different reasons. These reasons included: an incompatible school system that neither allowed me to study what interested me; nor would the school administration permit me to adjust my daily schedule to pursue figure skating by scheduling my day around available lower-cost ice time. I have known families who have selected home educate due to health concerns, bullying issues, learning needs, and specific intellectual pursuits. Yet unschooling remains an enigma to most, despite an overall increase in the number who are electing to home educate.

Recently, I've heard from home educating families how choosing unschooling really relieved much of the pressure they had felt. Instead of the daily struggle to find and follow a set curriculum, assign schoolwork, and create a functioning school-at-home environment, families quickly realize that education blossoms in the most surprising places and often doesn't involve pencils, paper or books at all. My mother knew that I would become bored if I had to sit still and complete pages and pages of homework assignments. She knew because my elementary school teachers during my three years in public school often assigned me extra credit work because I finished my regular assignments too quickly. My mother didn't think this was fair, that I should do twice the work, but didn't get a double grade or double credit, just because I learned quicker than others. Recognizing that school limited me, my mother decided to follow the unschooling approach. I am forever grateful to her for that decision. For me unschooling meant following whatever sparked my attention. I found that not spending my days in school meant I could do so much more.

Ultimately unschooling allowed me to work two part-time jobs, which helped me pay for a car when I learned to drive, helped me pay to continue my figure skating training when I was in my teens, allowed me to buy an electronic console piano to continue my piano studies, and helped me save to buy my own Mac computer. These were all things I wanted and used as elements in my own education, but coming from a lower income family, instead of relying on the schools to provide all my learning needs, I learned to set goals, figure out how to reach them, plan on how to earn the money I needed for whatever I wanted, then saved my money and bought the best value I could afford. We couldn't afford to buy a curriculum to use even if my parents had wanted to use one. My mom tried an online public school that touted its free curriculum, only to discover a long list of extremely annoying anomalies, like requiring a physical education credit, but not allowing me to fulfill this curricular credit with the three or more hours a day I spent on ice skating training. Each public, tax-supported approach we attempted disappointed and exasperated both me and my family. All the roadblocks and headaches ultimately led us back to unschooling.

In retrospect unschooling should have been the common sense choice from the beginning, allowing me the freedom to create my own academic goals while broadening my experiences. I taught myself how to design and construct patterns to sew my own clothing. I pushed myself as a competitive athlete, learning as much as possible about nutrition, training, conditioning and choreography, as well as designing and making my own skating outfits for performances. I taught myself algebra, geometry, trigonometry and calculus. For every challenge I faced I had family support, but I had to do the work myself, to reach my own goals.

In school someone hands the student a list of the books needed, the assignments to be read, the things he or she should learn; someone tells the students what and how to learn. What valuable life skills does one learn from that approach? I can tell you one: how to take directions. Most tests that students encounter throughout a lifetime of education insure that a student knows how to read instructions and follow them correctly. Teachers in most schools must insure that their students can do exactly that: follow instructions and only read what's in front of them. The message to the student is to do as one is told, to study what the school and the state have decided one should learn. Schools place limits on children, especially on their abilities and creativity. Schools also limit what skills a child learns. I don't blame teachers, since they seldom set these policies. The bureaucratic structure of our school systems is at fault. Take away the brick and mortar politics of school and you get home education. Remove the restrictions of a set curriculum and you discover unschooling. Measuring personal growth and intelligence shouldn't come from letter grades or tests geared toward one goal, proving a student can score within certain parameters on those tests. Why would we choose to define an individual's potential by how well that student can answer questions on tests, which mostly tests the student's reading and language art skills, rather than how well he or she can handle everyday life challenges? Why wouldn't we prefer to define intelligence by one's ability to apply experiences and knowledge to solve problems creatively, during the compulsory attendance years, then while in college, and later in one's workplace? A certain amount of inflexibility arises from the rigidity of institutionalized learning. Those who accept the mindset of only learning those things placed directly before them and only doing exactly what one is told to do will never take the risks necessary to reach full potential, because one cannot know one's full potential if one isn't free to discover just how far one can stretch one's abilities.

How might institutionalized learning adversely impact children? It often keeps them locked into a cookie cutter mold of what they can and cannot accomplish, focused on scoring well on state-mandated testing, often struggling with this testing and failing. Many students experience only failure from this type of testing and far too many simply give up completely, convinced that they can't learn anything. Some of those students will continue to associate learning and training situations with failure, well into adulthood, and will never pursue any post-secondary level education. Writing and spelling, for example, are skills no longer considered necessary to function in society. Too many look upon math and science as useless facts that will never apply to a student's life. Why should students learn algebra? Why should they learn how to spell? One doesn't need to know either algebra or spelling to get a job anymore. And in far too many cases one doesn't even need these skills to get accepted at a college. However, if a student can't learn basic mathematics and understand writing fundamentals, most colleges will require students to enroll in remedial courses. This not only extends the time it takes for students to earn a two or four-year degree, but the statistics for students who must enroll in remedial courses and who then complete a degree program are pretty grim. In fact only about one-third of students who start a bachelor's degree program in remedial classes for math and English will graduate within six years. And what about the other two-thirds who start with remedial classes? Most will not graduate at all, or will take many more years, often repeating courses, to complete a degree program, seriously increasing the cost of their "four-year" degree. If you do the math you can imagine the extra cost to the family or the individual due to just these two learning discrepancies. And don't count on the college or university to provide accurate information about this issue. As with all data, be sure to question what the college presents if it sounds unrealistically high. For example, the college I attended for my first two years listed an 85% graduation rate within the first five years, but, I must have known every single student in that 15% who didn't make it, because I was one of the only students at that college that I knew who finished in exactly four years.

I've seen many publicly educated students arrive at a university unprepared for college level classes who then find themselves overwhelmed by simultaneously taking both remedial and core curriculum classes. This immediately stresses those students, causing some to express anger at their pre-college schooling for not properly preparing them. Should all the blame be placed on the school for students who are failing? No. Parents play a huge role in any child's education. Unschooling requires both the presence and participation of the parent or parents. Not ready for the challenge of parenting and teaching? Then perhaps your child should continue to attend public school. What if you are a student and your parents aren't interested in helping you learn? I would try to find someone else who will help, even if that means remaining in school part-time if that options is available to you, and getting assistance from some teachers. Not every parent, family, or individual can handle the responsibility that comes with unschooling. All members of the family get involved in the choices unschoolers make: where to go, what books to read, what to study, how many hours a day one dedicates to any particular interest, and, of course, what activities the family can afford. All of these decisions require the full attention of the parents and the cooperation of the whole family unit.

Unschooling is not a spectator sport. Children don't get dropped off at a building and parents don't get six to eight hours a day, five days a week, of what my mom refers to as "tax-paid babysitting." And that's coming from someone who wanted to teach and who did teach for many years. My mother attended college early and started teaching high school English and French before she turned 21. But from her perspective, tax funded institutionalized schools will never change and will continue to simply provide daily care for some children, many whose parents don't really want them around all day. I know some will say that they simply can't afford the time, that they work multiple jobs, or are single parents, working long hours, etc. But, believe me, some single parents successfully home educate their children. Some families with both parents working manage to split homeschooling responsibilities, with both parents involved whenever they are not working.

Some families might find home educating impossible for them because of these kinds of work and family issues. Some may think that it takes too much money to do a good job as a home educator. But I've known some very low income families who did exceptionally well. I've seen very wealthy families, those from all different racial, religious and social backgrounds, home educate, too. Some choose unschooling and others choose to follow some type of prepackaged curriculum. I don't believe that one form of home education necessarily works better than another. Since no detailed statistics on these aspects of home education currently exist, I could never prove my theory on that either way. But I do know that I was unschooled and I thoroughly enjoy advocating the benefits of unschooling for all who elect to follow this course. In this book I talk about my experiences and how I transitioned from unschooling to college, then into adulthood and the workplace. I wanted to share my journey so that others might consider unschooling as a viable option. Consider this book a way to begin to know some of the facts about unschooling for those who might select this option, but who haven't found any good first-person accounts of what really goes on in the day-to-day life of an unschooler. In the same way, one doesn't just walk onto a car dealer's lot, point at a car, and buy it. Most smart shoppers research different cars, learn all they can about different models, test-drive the ones preferred, save for a down payment and look into financing options, find out about insurance rates, and then, finally, select a car, make a purchase offer. This book can assist those who would like to pursue an unschooling path, yet who also want to leave the door open to go to college and earn a specific degree. Also, I hope that with the help of this book everyone can discover more of his or her own potential. I want people to know the importance of creativity, self-expression, intelligence, and family. I feel that we all should support those qualities in our children today.

I've spent time tutoring and teaching. I've observed the pitfalls of the public school system firsthand, both as a child in the public schools and as an adult. For this book I researched the statistics on bullying, another factor that often leads families to choose home education. I know that peers can treat some school children horribly, often on a daily basis. I've read the headlines, seen the news stories, and watched the films on student suicides, school violence, and private school lotteries. I've spent the last two years working for an educational services company and I touch on all of these issues throughout this book. I'm not an expert, may not know everything about educational systems, but I am as much an expert on homeschooling as anyone, and on unschooling, or self-directed learning, in particular. In this book I have covered pretty much everything you need to know to unschool yourself or, if you're the parent, to unschool your child. You will also find facts and figures that often paint a less than attractive picture of the failings of our public schools. I hope that after reading this book more people will question their child's or children's education. I hope some will elect to exercise their right to educate their children at home and then choose unschooling. I even hope that some will fight for change in their schools to create better options for the future.

Ideally, I'd like to see public schools turned into amazing assets in our communities, producing more brilliant, happy, well adjusted students, who don't suffer from bullying and teasing and who don't grow up feeling like failures. Until that happens, though, I will voice my support for unschooling and home education.

# Orientation

*"Life is being wasted. The human family is not having half the fun that is its due, not making the beautiful things it would make, and each one is not as good news to the other as he might be, just because we are educated off our natural track. We need another form of education."-Robert Henri (Artist)*

    Walking down the street I resemble any other young person. Yet, my life story, how I grew into the person I am today, differs tremendously from that of my peers. Miraculously, in the eyes of many, I grew into a healthy and well adjusted adult. Contrary to popular belief, home education doesn't always create sheltered, religiously isolated individuals who can't function in society. In this book I will tell you how I matured into a socially adept young adult, with friends, a passion for success, and an overwhelming desire to educate and inspire people about the benefits of home education. This book will dispel many negative myths perpetuated by those who oppose home education and will also shed light on the inequalities and failures of some aspects of the public school system.

    From the age of eight until sixteen my life revolved around competitive figure skating. As a preteen I spent time volunteering for various organizations. To save money for my first car, I worked part time at a public library and worked as a salesclerk at a local museum facility. During my teen years I attended school dances and proms with friends who went to public and private schools. On weekends I went to movies, pretended to play pool, and tried to defeat my friends at the card game "Spoons." I stayed out too late, attended parties and threw some of my own parties. When the time arrived to decide about college, I prepared for and took the ACT and SAT exams and sent out my admissions and scholarship applications, crossing my fingers for acceptance and a full tuition scholarship. Just like most of my friends, I attended college and graduated in the spring of 2010 with a four year Bachelor of Arts degree. The only difference between me and my friends was that from the age of 10 until I left for college, I didn't attend school. And, as it turned out, I ended up "not attending" my last two years of college. I transferred to a college with an excellent online degree program that I found much more creative and interdisciplinary, exactly what I wanted, instead of the residential college program I first entered and attended for my freshman and sophomore years.

I remember my brief public school experience as one of stress, disappointment, shunning and loneliness. My female peers, who were busy fighting over best friend status with the most popular girl, often resorted to cruelly teasing or shunning me from conversations and activities. I never understood why we couldn't all be best friends with each other. In public school the predefined hierarchical status, one that grows only more cruel and intense throughout the middle school and high school years, remains consistent and active. Popularity and social status, no matter what the cost, no matter if it destroys the self esteem of someone else, no matter if it causes physical or emotional damage, remain social priorities in the school hallways. Honestly, my experiences were very mild compared to the horrible bullying occurring in some schools today. While on public school property, or sometimes on buses or walking home from school, both boys and girls can find themselves the targets of bullies, harassed, teased, taunted and sometimes physically and sexually assaulted.

I've read news story after news story in which parents stated how helpless they felt, how they didn't know how else they could protect their child. Parents often ask schools for help and come away frustrated, disillusioned, and disappointed by the school's lack of action. Why do parents feel they have no other choice than to put up with their child being humiliated and berated every day that he or she walks into a school building?  Social convention convinces parents that they have no other choice, that attending public school will be the best for their child's future and education.  This is not the truth, though.  I hope that after reading this book more families will realize that not only can they offer better home education options, better academic and creative freedom, but also that families and students can escape the horrible social suffering often encountered in public school.

Often I've wanted to lie about being home educated.  Sometimes I've felt like I'm wearing a big scarlet letter "H," or that maybe I should be.  Interestingly, some of my biggest lessons came from finding the strength to embrace the amazing opportunities home education gave me and to wear my scarlet "H" proudly.  Growing older has shown me that people claiming they are "well adjusted," or who believe home educated students are inferior to them, often turn out to be the most socially insecure and/or maladjusted people I've met.  I've observed that many who were bullies in high school remain bullies as adults.

For me, writing this book has been a deeply personal experience because my educational choices reflect so much about me and my goals, my dreams, my hopes for the future.  I hope that you, the reader, will come away from this book with a different perspective on home education. Filling the blank pages on a computer screen with the trials and tribulations of my home education years was not an easy task; rather it was one that took years to bring to fruition.  I hope at the very least readers will find my book insightful.  One of the main goals for writing this book stems from my opinion that compulsory attendance, traditional institutionalized learning, fosters a culture of people who discover the benefits of manipulation, bullying, lying, cheating and stealing.  I believe that public schools teach students how to get by with the minimum required for grades, success, and the skills necessary to function in everyday life.  Shunning, shaming, coercing, and stereotyping are normal and accepted behaviors within the confines of many classroom environments. Such a lack of concern for each other, as well as lack of knowledge beyond the four walls of a school, fosters generations of young people who continue to perpetuate self-destructive behavior, often well into adulthood.

The public school environment educates students to achieve a certain level of knowledge specified by boards and bureaucracies and does not educate the individual on moral obligations or responsibilities, such as empathy or concern for peers and for our communities. Nor does the school endow the student with any sense of personal values, instead often demoralizing the individual to such a degree that all sense of right or wrong, personal expression, and the ability to think for one's self gets destroyed. These students learn how to function solely when given explicit instructions on what they must learn and how they should think. If concerned about the effectiveness of learning, look no further than how much more an unschooled or home schooled student can learn, by focusing on specific learning goals, then following up and applying lessons learned to the real world.

In school test scores trump everything else and dominate all other goals, surpassing other more meaningful ideals. Public schools educate students using a system of testing, measuring knowledge through arduous test booklets and assessments. Public schools educate students on how to conform, on how to determine their self-worth based on arbitrary numbers and letter grades. Primarily public schools educate children about either hopelessness or hopefulness. Should the student fall into the hopeless category, he or she will learn to fear education because education taught them that learning sets up a slippery slope that can carry them upwards, but can also swiftly roll them back down. Further, he or she will often decide not to trust, enjoy nor explore learning any more than necessary to pass required tests.

I'd like my book to be an example of how alternative education nurtures the individual and sustains a lifelong desire to learn. Everyone knows that life challenges us. So parents who want their children around, who want to facilitate learning because they enjoy learning themselves, could change the future of education, of invention and imagination, offering hope for a brighter future. Alright, maybe I'm being a little melodramatic. But, how will you know? Did Albert Einstein know that his inventive thinking would alter the world as he knew it? Honestly, more often than not I've felt like I'm never doing enough. I should be doing this, or that; I should have accomplished more by now; sound familiar? My mom can tell you about the many times that I've cried and stated, completely convinced, that I have failed at life or just wasn't smart enough. Life can screw with your head, and even a completely emotionally stable, successful, and happy child can feel like there's a fail sign stamped on his or her forehead. Even a home educated student can feel at odds with his or her education. Nothing is perfect.

Surely those in school have felt many of the same things I've felt and I can't imagine feeling like this while walking through cold, institutional hallways in school, surrounded by my peers, who are more likely to judge than console or consider others. Have you felt like a failure, or are you a parent who has a child who has felt like this? Maybe you've heard in the news about the bullying and teen suicide rate, and wonder what the schools are doing about this sort of thing or are you the sort of person who considers that to be lame or wimpy? Maybe you survived your school days fine, despite being teased, tormented, and taunted. If you survived all right, then why can't your kid? Unlike you, kids today use the Internet, cell phones, social networking, etc, to exaggerate and spread every possible tease, taunt and humiliation to unbearable degrees. Does "sexting" sound familiar to anyone? The public school landscape can trip up the best of students with its veritable minefield of potential verbal, emotional or physical attacks.

When I was a kid the worst thing I endured was some bratty kid who called me "curly buckteeth." Honestly, who wants children to hear that kind of comment about themselves every day that they walk into a school building? The entire school structure fosters alienation, abuse, anger and frustration. To create change parents must embrace a better approach to education. However, that demands more work, time and energy than simply dropping the kids off in front of a school building. Home education requires sacrifice and dedication. Not every family can home educate and home education is not for everyone. But despite that, everyone can extract from this book the understanding that with home education all learning prevails well beyond the classroom. Everyone can actively participate, can teach, even if only by example.

Before compulsory schooling children learned from experiences at home, from their parents, siblings, extended families and every home was the school; every field, every room, and every day brought new lessons. I think that system worked well. History yields many famous home educated figures: Albert Einstein, President Abraham Lincoln, Leonardo da Vinci, John Quincy Adams, George Washington, Moses, Joan of Arc, Booker T. Washington, C.S. Lewis, Hans Christian Anderson, Leo Tolstoy, Ansel Adams, Florence Nightingale, Mark Twain, Charles Dickens, Agatha Christie. Do I really need to keep going?

I might be a bit of a dreamer, but I know in my heart that the schools of today will, more often than not, stifle generations of future inventors, innovators and artists from reaching the success that they might otherwise have achieved. In today's society the successful, wealthy and philanthropic people, for the most part, attend private, highly exclusive preparatory schools before going on to run successful businesses. Some systems of education work better than others. Consider home education as another form of education that can foster high-level intellectual and creative development in students.

The real problem with public education stems from a lack of responsibility. When did parents start feeling incapable of educating their own children, or at least providing supplemental resources and support? Too many parents have stopped wanting to take responsibility for their children, the tender souls that they have chosen to bring into this world. Mothers and fathers stick a backpack on the child's back, stuff some food in his or her lunch pail and say, "Hey, you, stranger; yeah, you in the big building, you will now teach my kid everything that he or she needs to know."

In a classroom with 20-30, or more, other students, a child could never learn everything he or she needs to know, nor can a child even learn all those things a teacher attempts to instruct. Everything that can be learned and taught will never fit in the limited selection of books available in too many underfunded schools. Deep wells of knowledge exist in our communities, in the experiences of a nation and in the cultures of the world. Learning builds the foundation for survival and success. Finding the education needed comes from surprising and not so surprising places, like the color of the flowers in a garden, colors that were created through evolutionary processes that allow the flower to better attract pollinators, or for the flower to attract sources of food, like the carnivorous Venus fly trap, for example.

Knowledge populates the shelves of libraries, Internet web resources, kitchens, and stores. Think of shopping trips that involve calculating how much an item costs using unit pricing on store shelves, or how much a 20% discount will save you. Everything each individual needs to know awaits the excitement of discovery every day. Someone only needs to guide or nudge the student toward the information, and then allow the student to apply the information, allowing the student to learn. The one true gift society can give to children, is not just an education, but true inner knowledge.

Who I am today and how I arrived here, how my unschooled journey began, originated with my passion for ice skating and was supported by my mother's devotion and love. With both of these I began on a path which has forever changed my life. Through my family's dedication to my success, by giving of themselves, sharing their time and knowledge, as well as sparse financial resources, my parents helped me realize the importance of setting goals. I've learned how to think, something very underrated in much of today's world. I realized it's not about how far the journey takes you, it's about what happens along the way. For me making the decision to create my life around my interests opened doors, doors that have led to opportunities I never expected. Home education allowed me the time and the flexibility to explore the rooms, places and people beyond those doors.

Individual motivation for choosing home education can vary greatly. For some the decision arises for religious or health related reasons. Some parents are strongly compelled to educate their children following a specific philosophical doctrine. Others choose home education for the sake of the emotional and physical well-being of the child. Many families, however, don't realize that home education exists as a choice for them. Public educators often instill fear in parents, fear that what parents might try to provide themselves would shortchange the student. Recently a parent was sent a waiver form to sign, which is not part of our state's laws on home education, in which the parents were to sign off, indicating that they are foregoing an appropriate education for their child by requesting to register as a home educator. Of course they realize that a first-time home educating parent would be forced to reconsider when faced with this type of waiver. Administrators of public school systems want parents to believe that compulsory attendance is the only credible way for a child to learn properly. What does learning properly even mean? What is an "appropriate education"? Can a teacher write a plethora of facts on a chalk or white board, geared to get students to pass a state assessment test? Yes, of course a teacher can do exactly that. Any teacher can stand in front of a group of children, take a piece of chalk and write a fact on a board, or open a book and read aloud more facts, vainly attempting to keep the attention of the young minds in the classroom. Is that considered an appropriate education? Should that even be considered an education? Do those actions define education? Do those actions represent a proper education? Sounds a little delusional to truly believe that every teacher in every classroom has the proper skill set to educate every child placed in his or her classroom. In most states teachers in public schools are de facto restricted to preparing children for the sole purpose of passing state mandated assessment exams. Anything beyond these exams merits only limited attention. Want to learn about chemistry while in grade school? Want to create an experiment? Build an electric race car? Learn how a plane flies? Understand the cocooning metamorphosis of a caterpillar? Unless these items appear on the assessment, that student will probably not learn about it. Teachers are limited by a bureaucratically controlled system almost entirely motivated by statistical requirements and financial limitations.

Will a student in school who loves learning and enjoys to learn receive the encouragement he or she needs? Maybe, but very unlikely. Will he or she receive the emotional support necessary for success in school from a teacher with thirty or more other students? No, teachers are not paid to be surrogate parents, contrary to popular belief. Teachers usually go home to their own families and lives. Expecting parents and schools to attend to every need of every child places an enormous burden on peers and teachers, often fostering bullying behavior, or facilitating it. Parents convinced that the public school will protect his or her child from harm, because that's the school's job, may discover that this was never the intent of the public school system.

Originally public schools were devised to educate people just enough, so that they could work in factory positions during the Industrial Revolution. The main goal? Educate the mass population to at least read and write, do basic "ciphering," and increase production. At that time a college education was only available to children from wealthy families and they usually attended private preparatory institutions. That original mentality remains much the same, despite expanding availability to the masses and opening up higher learning to more than just the entitled elite. Public schools still offer little more than they always did and students who attend them still struggle with academic and financial requirements necessary to attend college.

Everyday children step onto a crowded school bus, attend a public school under the pretense of receiving an appropriate education. Everyday parents entrust a public school to do exactly that, while also ensuring the safety and well being of millions of children. On the school bus ride some children will enjoy a relatively pleasant, albeit long and boring ride to their school, but many will face threats and physical abuse, shoving, punching, choking, yelling, name-calling and cursing at the hands of other students on the bus. In some areas middle school and high school students ride the same bus as much younger children. For the younger students the fear of riding on the bus, facing the harassment of older or bigger students, will make each morning's wait for the bus feel like Russian roulette. Will I be punched today? Will I be choked? Will someone try to steal my lunch money? What am I doing wrong to make others try to hurt me? Those are all questions a child in this situation will ask while his or her parents could be completely oblivious to what's happening. Why? Children don't want to worry an already overstressed and exhausted parent. Maybe the child has never seen his or her father or mother cry, and that child, the one who struggles with bullying, feels weak and pathetic because of his or her own weakness and remains quiet about these all too common problems.

Children silently suffer and some will remain silent until it's too late to discover the truth. In the United States too many sweet, loving, dedicated and empathetic children, some as young as 11, have taken their own lives, unable to continue to suffer the abuse forced upon them by other students. Parents often feel completely helpless, unable to do anything. Some parents may be totally unaware of what is happening at school, since schools only report incidents witnessed by a school employee or reported directly to them by a student. Everyday a child will struggle, will cry, and will hurt. Everyday a parent will wonder what else he or she can do. Where can he or she find help? Why can't the school do more? When will the school do more? Why won't the school protect my child? Stop asking these questions. Each day that a parent gives up hope, a parent could be deciding a child's future. Home education doesn't create uneducated children, home education gives hope to many of those bright, beautiful children who deserve better. Stop allowing children to suffer through an unworthy and unkind education, an education that fails to acknowledge the individual needs of each child.

Step out toward progress. If public schools are truly the best for the future of children, why are students increasingly required to take remedial math and remedial writing courses in college after completing twelve years in public school education? Why do parents in cities like New York pay $120 an hour for tutors to get their preschoolers prepped for elite private preschools, so that their children can attend even more elite private prep schools or public schools for gifted and talented students only? Because they know that regular public schools will not provide a good enough education for their children to succeed, gain admission to a good college, earn scholarships. If public education worked the way everyone believes it does, if it worked properly then you'd see more students graduating, more intelligent, creative, and caring individuals entering their adult lives and careers. Instead test scores continue to fall.

Fewer and fewer students can complete college in just four years. Suicide is now the third highest cause of death for children ages 10-14 and the second highest cause of death for teenagers and young adults 15-24. Now ask yourself, do you still believe public schools are properly fulfilling their job? If they are then why do students continue to struggle with the basics of reading, writing and mathematics? Why are students so depressed and reporting bullying nearly every day? Public schools will never give a child a safe and strong education. American students are failing. Bullying dominates the lives of some students and will never disappear from the public school environment, an environment that feeds the very seeds of bullying. Parents must step up and take a stand. Students must demand something better. Remaining hopeless and silent is no longer acceptable.

I believe the doors to many possibilities and opportunities exist for every child and that the greatest of minds, our nation's future philosophers, humanitarians, and intellectuals, may not escape the limitations and sufferings of our public education system. Jobs, friendships, experiences, personal realizations and inner growth blossom, form, and strengthen the individual outside of the classroom. All of these things have nurtured the person I have become today. Choosing to unschool or home educate is not a decision to be taken lightly. Deciding to follow an alternative educational path opens many doors to many different possibilities that will reveal themselves over time. Most importantly, choosing to unschool means believing that you and your child have immeasurable potential for growth, even if it only begins with something as simple as a pair of ice skates, or a love for bugs, or an interest in paleontology. Who knows where these interests or inspirations may lead, but how amazing would it feel to witness the blossoming, the evolution of even one individual student?

My pair of ice skates led me down the path to become an unschooled student, a role model, a teacher, a college student, a college grad, and now an author. Looking back, I'm amazed how much learning flows naturally, without force, without definition, without the need for rigid curricular walls. Trying to define education often simply limits all that it can be. I know that fostering a system that does not individualize learning limits the potential success for far too many children. I believe that the flexibility and fluidity of home education can nurture individuals who become successful, intelligent and empathetic human beings, those who will someday redefine the idea of education, individuals like me.

# De-schooling

*"Whatever an education is, it should make you a unique individual, not a conformist; it should furnish you with an original spirit with which to tackle the big challenges; it should allow you to find values which will be your road map through life; it should make you spiritually rich, a person who loves whatever you are doing, wherever you are, whomever you are with; it should teach you what is important, how to live and how to die." – John Taylor Gatto*

     To openly approach home education one must first de-school. Yes, I'll admit it's not in the dictionary. The prefix "de-" denotes removal or reversal. In this case "de-schooling," means removal of schooling, or reversal of schooling. Schools are the institutions or buildings in which children are educated, but are children honestly learning in these buildings? In home education the tangible brick and mortar structure no longer exists. What a terrifying thought for someone thinking about home education: to educate without set boundaries, rules, or classroom structures. In the realm of home education, one must forge ahead into extremely murky and unknown waters. To quote a song by Bird York: "Now you're out there swimming in the deep." From my point of view that sounds like an amazing and beautiful adventure. How about you? Are you ready to swim in the deep? Are you prepared to not know all the correct answers? Life doesn't supply an answer key or cheat sheet and neither does learning. In the world of home education one must erase the images of school from one's mind. That large building with wide hallways and classrooms full of posters, pencils, and ringing bells does not exist in home education. From here on out you, the person, fulfill the role of educator, no longer constrained by assessments, red tape, time requirements, or rigid schedules.

Take a breath and spend a moment to realize the potential. As you decompress, you can now consider a plethora of possibilities. Perhaps you will discover that home education throws open the doors of learning possibilities ever wider, introducing rooms and realms full of new and interesting prospects. Without the static classroom and desk a child can learn from a multitude of resources, attend a greater variety of classes or activities, and spend a greater amount of time learning. Instead of listening to lectures on topics usually presented solely for test preparation, students can involve themselves in learning about living life. Imagine a morning, without rushing to get children off to school, when a child can begin his or her own personalized study program. He or she could continue a previous project from the day before, tune into an educational show on television, begin studying a new topic, attend a theatrical performance, or visit a museum.

Children instinctively want to learn; they enjoy challenges and they strive to build upon previous knowledge in new and interesting ways. Many children and adults spend hours playing video and computer games. Designers of these games realize the compulsion and satisfaction of defeating opponents and completing levels that increase in difficulty. Without this increase a game player gets bored. This explains why gaming companies are constantly supplying game players with expansion packs that offer more levels with more difficult challenges. Often expansion packs appear to be coincidentally timed for release precisely when the average player will lose interest in the game.

Surprisingly, schools are completely unaware of this simple idea upon which gaming companies capitalize and profit. Not only do these games draw in many children, but adults also get caught up in the apparent never-ending desire for constant mental and visual stimulation that these games offer. For the home educating individual this stimulation can be part of his or her education.

Realizing that home education can satisfy the need for challenge, the need to engage the whole person in learning activities will help develop the true potential that any child can reach. When school fails to adequately challenge a student the student will often seek other forms of stimulation. Many of these other forms of stimulation satisfy a student in the short term, but in the long term only distract the child from the fact that his or her life lacks a significant or meaningful sense of challenge.

Stimulating children's minds with something more productive than video games opens up amazing learning opportunities. Don't think it's possible? Have you looked at those games? Honestly, if the student realized the complexities and excitement possible in real life challenges, they would probably walk away from their game consoles, even if only for a few hours. When one is de-schooling one recognizes that school often fails to intellectually challenge students and only minimally motivates them. For a child who craves challenges, school may loom on the horizon, unattractive, unappealing, a wasteland. Instead of suggesting that children should feel less intelligent because school doesn't satisfy or stimulate them, perhaps we could admit that most of these students simply desire more appropriate challenges. Public education lays out a one-size-fits-all approach to learning. Just as it may not encourage teachers to focus on their own strengths and experiences, it may also fail to adequately recognize the individual strengths or weaknesses of each student. Thus many teachers aren't honestly facing their own shortcomings. For those who are considering the alternative of unschooling, or self-directed learning, prepare yourself to first reconcile the idea of reversing, reconsidering, and acknowledging the flaws in the typical brick and mortar school environment, especially if you already know you don't have a one-size-fits-all child.

Push aside the image of school, the stories you've heard about home education, and the ideals sold to you about the public school system. Whatever apprehensions you might have, you must first move past them, for you are going against the flow, like a salmon swimming upstream. First and foremost, you are de-schooling yourself. Questions and criticism will continually arise over the course of this home education journey, questions from you, from your student, and questions from others. Remain positive and focused on the importance of providing a nurturing and supportive education. Open your mind to all that education can be, instead of what you've been told it should be.

Are you a parent who already home educates your child or children, or are you considering it? Are you a young person interested in home education? Maybe you are a family member or friend of someone who is involved in home education? Whatever might have enticed you to read this book, this is your moment to breathe. Consider where you are right now. Are you happy with what you've seen or experienced while you or your child was in the public school system? Do you wonder about other options? Are you trying to decide what you want and now feel completely overwhelmed, unsure, confused? That's good. You are feeling exactly what you should feel. Most parents send children to school without much thought. They walk their children to the bus, or down the street, and they are gone most of the day. Easy-peasy. No thought process required, job done, you have fulfilled the truancy laws in your state.

To create a true learning environment, on the other hand, will encompass work and dedication. That's why you're possibly freaking out a little. Maybe you're nervous that a family member will ask a million annoying questions about the effectiveness of home education, or express concerns about home education. Nearly everyone you meet will strongly advocate the importance of attending traditional school. For whatever reasons, no matter who asks those trying questions, feel free to wonder, to consider a different choice. Investigate as long as you need, a moment or a few moments, to explore all your options. Deciding to educate your children at home, or to unschool them, could be one of the most difficult, as well as one of the most exciting and satisfying life-altering decisions you will ever consider. Spend as much time as you need to truly appreciate what will work best for everyone involved.

Critics would persuade you otherwise, stressing all the reasons why you should not even consider home education, let alone unschooling or self-directed learning. Those who oppose home education often spread misguided, misinformed, and sometimes hateful or judgmental opinions on this subject. But have any of those people presented any hard facts that prove why you shouldn't home educate or unschool your child or children? I'm almost 100% sure that no such proof exists. What one hears from most critics of home education frequently stems from personal opinions or biases, not fact. During the early phase of de-schooling, you must allow yourself the opportunity to first learn and better understand home education. Don't stress about considering this choice. Listen to your gut, to your inner voice, before you decide. Trust that you are capable, that you can handle both your own education and that of your family.

When a deep sea diver rises to the surface after a dive, he or she must ascend carefully. Come up too fast and the pressure change will precipitate the bends, causing the diver to feel sick. Same goes for this home education decision; don't jump into this decision too fast. Don't let others stress you out because you are diving into the deep end and will need to come up for air at your own pace. Those who judge, pressure, and create undue stress do not hold your best interests at heart. Instead they want you to surface faster, force you to focus on their ideas.

Instead you must decompress, breathe, de-stress, and approach the whole idea of home education and unschooling from a relaxed perspective. Take it slowly, discuss home education with as many people as possible, read, research, ask questions, and join home education support groups. In this way you will decompress and no longer feel so stressed about what you are facing. Read as many books as possible about home education. Get involved in a home education forum, on online blog, local support groups or online e-groups. Ask lots of questions and form your own ideas about what you'd like to achieve through home education, what you expect, and what you most fear. List all the things you'd like to know. Consider costs for transportation to classes or activities outside the home, or for other things usually provided by a school. Ask yourself if you can truly handle the amazing opportunity of having a child around you all the time at home. If you're a young person, will your family accept that you prefer to stay home? How will you establish a plan that clearly defines what and how you will fulfill your educational and personal objectives, one that spells out the goals you prefer to pursue? Home education is not a spectator sport. Once you step out onto the field it's very difficult to remove yourself from the game. So, ruminate over all the issues, write ideas down, and ask questions before you decide on your home education plan. Even though when some people think homeschooled they immediately conjure up images of religious radicals who focus solely on their religious teachings all day, you should understand that home education preceded all other current forms of education, especially institutionalized education. And you will no more find that all homeschoolers are religious radicals than you will find that homeschoolers are bunch of hippies sitting around doing macramé all day.

If you think about it, public education might be the more radical approach. For centuries children learned in the home, from family, or tutors, or from hands-on experiences. The traditional classroom setting simply wasn't available for any but the very rich, the most elite. Many people will support the view that the right to a public education revolutionized learning and establishes a fair opportunity for all children to participate. Ignore those people. There is nothing "fair" about our educational system today when some schools are quite literally falling apart. Some suffer from hazardous materials in the school buildings and grounds, while others sport indoor pools with slides.

Slow down so that you can completely understand what home education entails. Not only will the time you spend with your children, with your family, increase tenfold, but so will the potential for frustration and exhaustion. I didn't write this book as a soap box to convince people that everyone should select home education. I wrote this book to educate people about an alternative to the accepted norm from my first-person point of view. That's why I want you to truly step back a bit and consider your personal situation before choosing home education or, more specifically, unschooling. Spread everything out on the table and clear the way for your decisions. Don't miss this step, because once you commence your own home education journey you will be up to your eyeballs in all kinds of day-to-day decisions. And, believe it or not, that's when the real fun will start.

To plunge into de-schooling certain paradigms must shift, completely altering your perspective on education. Don't begin home education with any expectations. Doing so perpetuates the mindset that home education and public education parallel each other, strive for the same goals. Believing this furthers the illusion that home education should, at least in some respects, replicate institutionalized learning. If you fail to de-school yourself then you'll struggle to embrace all that home education can offer. Think of it as the difference between taking the clearly marked path or forging your own path on "the road less traveled." When you stick with the same ideals found in the public school system you only detract from the potential inspiration possible with home education. In school the ideals revolve around achieving definable goals through letter grades and test scores. Defining something this way creates quantitative limitations. When you step outside the mindset of what school means to everyone else, you can redefine the goals of your life. By this I mean that you can define your own potential and intellectual accomplishments by what you do, create, design, grow, or change, instead of by numbers or letters scrawled on pieces of paper.

Home education liberates the student, inspiring each one to think his or her own individual thoughts and to motivate him or herself through unique projects based on personal passions. While schools offer a limited menu of simple and barely palatable required classes, home education expands one's options all the way through the compulsory schooling years. I understood that students are only allowed to pick their own classes in high school. But what about younger children? Who says an 8 year old doesn't know what he or she would like to study? Recently my mom met a brilliant 8 year old who knew exactly what interested him and could have chattered to her for hours about it. We impose extremely controlling restrictions on what a child can learn and when a student can learn certain things. What if someone had tried to tell Einstein what to learn and when? I'm sure we'd live in a very different world. Want to know a secret? The public school model has conditioned us to accept that the age of a child determines his or her capabilities and intelligence. In each grade every child attending public school, as well as most private and parochial schools, will take assessment or achievement tests to gauge how much he or she memorized over the course of the school year.

Every state poses different guidelines for whichever questions students must answer on these tests and the standards, or rubrics, used to score those questions. Usually rooms full of teachers serving on committees create the test prompts and the rubrics for scoring these prompts. Since these teachers never personally take the tests they design, they often fail to consider the biases, format issues, or confusion a question might cause for a student. No matter how much consideration goes into the formulation of a single test question, an assessment test will never accurately gauge the abilities of every child. Instead assessment tests mostly gauge a child's aptitude for reading and following directions. This is not exactly a good way to recognize a child's strengths and weaknesses, nor to foster his or her personal potential.

A group of people you'll never meet and who will never meet the children taking the tests decide what children should learn in public schools. No one will probably ask the student how well he or she understood the test. So every spring children across the country take tests that sometimes totally fail to increase learning, since no one discusses the results with the child or the parents. No one sits down and goes over each question, and the score the child received for each question, so that everyone can learn from the experience of taking these tests. Nonetheless, these tests can determine whether or not a child can matriculate to the next grade. Do we honestly want the future success of a child to be based on a simple test that can dramatically vary in rigor and format from one state to another? Assessment tests will never provide clear or valid insight into the academic potential of a child. If these tests could achieve this goal, then public schools wouldn't fail so many students.

In recent years the popularity of charter schools continues to increase and now families applying to them face long waiting lists to get in and sit apprehensively through lottery sessions, hoping that their number gets chosen. What's the draw to a charter school, some run entirely by foreign staff and teachers in the US? It's the success of the students, of course. Charter schools tend to yield higher graduation rates and a higher number of students who attend college. If traditional public schools could achieve those two things families wouldn't desperately attempt to enroll their children in alternative learning institutions. Doesn't seem like much to ask, right? What more could we hope for than students who can graduate and go on to college?

De-schooling involves breaking free from the delusion that public education creates the perfect learning environment. Going against the typical convention of following the crowd, home education encourages individuals to decide and think for themselves, fostering individual strength, patience, and dedication. By reading this book you are considering the potential an alternative education can offer to you, your child, and everyone else in your family. Already you're stronger than you realize because it takes strength to think for yourself. Going against the flow looks and feels difficult, but everyday nature demonstrates how to do this with astounding results. Just as salmon swim upstream, life thrives in the deepest and darkest crevices of the ocean, and amazing things arise in unexpected places. Should one consider home education, or maybe even the more "provocative" unschooling, then swimming against the current will become commonplace. Anticipate many questions to arise, for example:

"What will I need to learn?"

"As a parent, what should I provide for my child?"

"As a home educated student or unschooled student what resources lead to chances for further individual growth?"

Note that I'm not saying, "how" will I learn. The majority of children gain knowledge if given the opportunity and support. No one asks how that student will read a book, or how that student will write a paper. They ask the student what he or she is reading or writing. Will your student study algebra? Maybe calculus? What will he or she need to prepare for college? What to learn involves thought and planning. Start asking the important questions early in the de-schooling process. Determine goals, and soon you will be discussing the myriad possibilities of education, instead of the struggles. Each day an unschooled student can create a new project, visit the library, discover an interesting book, perhaps a book not assigned on a reading list. Maybe he or she will pursue a passion for robots, the galaxy, or an athletic discipline like gymnastics, dance, or ice skating. Rather than spending a whole day sitting in school, with every minute rigidly arranged around sometimes superfluous activities, an unschooled student may decide how to spend each hour, each minute, of each day.

Between the ages of eight and sixteen I chose to dedicate four hours of my typical day to figure skating. For those eight years every choice I made revolved around figure skating and I loved every moment. With every fall, every new challenge, I was always learning. Through falling I learned to always get back up and try again and again. With every new spin, or jump, or turn to master I realized that perseverance and practice pay off. No one told me that figure skating came with so many lessons, and not just the ones taught by my coaches, but also the ones that inspired me, built my confidence and strengthened my body. I didn't know from that first step on the ice how figure skating would contribute to my future or lead me to decide to organize and run a learn-to-skate program, observing how a small business functions while developing the confidence to speak before a group and instruct groups of both children and adults.

On the map of home education all roads lead to new experiences and personal journeys, unlike the limited roads the public schooled student travels that often revolve around a stationary building. Unfold the potential of home education as if exploring the map of a new place with a variety of directions in which one can travel. Like planning a trip and following the squiggly lines from one destination to another, each new line your finger traces represents a cornucopia of chances to grow and explore. Imagine home education and unschooling as an edgeless map of learning. Locations transform from dots into real life moments in which one can meet new people, gather previously unknown information and further expand a student's knowledge. All those lines laid out in a maze of colors now exist not simply as posters on a classroom wall, but as paths toward imagination, creativity and intellectual stimulation.

Public schools value the daily shuffle of class to class, room to room, class to playground. Structure as the utmost precedent focuses on a single road to travel from kindergarten through 12th grade. How do you reach your full potential when the road before you already exists, is already completely planned out? How will you know how far you can go or where you might end up when the map you're following only maps one route? Ask yourself, do you truly only want go down the "road most traveled" when instead you can embrace the potential experiences and freedom to expand your knowledge without limitations through a self-motivated and individualized educational path? Self-motivation leads to innovation and creativity, characteristics difficult to nurture in a traditional school environment.

If one is simply answering questions on a board or on a test sheet in a classroom, how can anyone learn any more than the content required to respond to those questions? Unschooling creates questions like: "What can I study today; what opportunities for growth are available this week; how much information will I collect, learn, or share?" Ask these questions every day and enjoy how the answers change from one day to the next, from one week or year to the next. Responses to questions for the unschooled student are open for discussion, negotiation or adjustment, based on the ever-changing kaleidoscope of life goals. One day you will start asking yourself: "What will I do with my life?" Looking back you will notice that you have already accomplished so much, having planted many learning seeds in the very fertile ground of your mind, and that your future hangs ripe on the vine.

Even young children wonder about the purpose of life. Adults may still be asking themselves this question after years of raising children, going to work, and then retiring. Everyone must deal with the decision about what to do in life. For a home educating or unschooling student deciding can begin early. In the early teens an unschooler can take college courses and receive college credit long before their peers are even thinking about college. Whereas the student who follows a set curriculum in an institutionalized school will usually graduate between the ages of 18-19, attend college for four years, possibly go on to grad school. Home educated students may choose to attend college as early as 14 or 15, or sometimes younger, depending on the restrictions set by the university or college they choose. (Read my chapter, "So what about college?" to learn how an unschooled and home educated student can easily attend college). Will you or your child go to college? Will that be what you do with your life? If so, then start asking the right questions early, compiling information and researching. Of course attending college isn't the only path for a home educated student. Plenty of other possibilities might arise, such as working in the family business, becoming an author, artist, musician, truck driver, inventor, entrepreneur, etc.

In my case I wanted to be a famous ice skater. I never achieved that dream, but that didn't matter because along the way I learned discipline, focus, and how to overcome challenges, fears, how to handle pressure and judgment. Now as an adult I can deal with these issues when they arise. Unschooled and home educated students can design flexible schedules around personal needs, so that they can nurture a wide array of subjects and interests. Some of my interests required years of dedication, others only a few weeks, such as an art class. I'm still deciding what I will do with my life, and it changes from day to day sometimes. However, unschooling gave me the confidence to consider pursuing challenging goals and dreams. I've followed passions and pursuits unavailable and/or unfamiliar to my publicly schooled peers. Whatever I select, I have chosen to live passionately, opening my mind to new ideas, all because I opened it to the remarkable journey of unschooling. You have to fight, balk the mainstream to create a life and an education full of potential for joy and success.

As part of the de-schooling experience, hopefully one realizes that schools can't provide all the answers. Schools will threaten parents, insisting that most parents don't have the authority, skills, or education to teach their own children. They will bully you and tell you that you're doing more harm than good to your child. Please don't believe them. When dedicated parents balk the bureaucracy of our public schools and challenge the authority of so-called experts, all kinds of good things can happen. Parents can change the schools in a multitude of ways; schools don't improve solely on their own. Look at our schools today in which many children can not read or write. Don't believe me? Try visiting an inner city school or a rural school district. I've tutored in a city school and have seen how children struggle to learn math, writing and reading. Choose something better. Fight for something better; if not unschooling then at least challenge the school system. Because having children in an industrial nation who cannot read or write, who fail to gain facility with simple everyday math, is unacceptable. Don't let your child settle for the same fate as millions of other children.

Unschooling might not fit every family. If you never change your thinking about education, then you'll never know what might work. Simply going along, pretending that everything is alright should no longer be an option. Too many children are punished for just wanting to learn, for wanting to be heard. If you keep thinking that public schools will always make the right decision for the education of children, then you are contributing to the problem. In a fair and equal world all children would receive the same caliber of education in clean, safe buildings, staffed with dedicated, caring and prepared teachers. That ideal doesn't exist and most likely never will. Too many people are taking advantage of the educational disparities today. Too many people believe that only certain children are capable and intelligent enough to receive college degrees. Public schools can belittle and subjugate children, making them feel like failures.

      When teachers suffer from overwork, intense stress, inadequate pay, and can't handle a classroom of 20-30 students, then schools cannot ensure a fair and equal education for every student. Nor can they assure the safety of every student. The standard 1:30 ratio in a typical public school classroom equates to a complete lack of personal one-on-one time for students. Only the noisiest and most persistent students will always manage to get attention, usually at the expense of others. Those quiet students, too shy, too ashamed, too afraid to try, will never find the necessary support needed, except perhaps from a parent willing to educate that child at home. So, if children need their parents for success in school anyway, why maintain school as the intermediary? If you're already doing most of the work, like reviewing your child's homework every night, then stop letting the schools control what happens to your child between the hours of 8:00 a.m. and 4:00 p.m. Take back control. If anyone holds the keys to understanding and working one-on-one with students, it would be the parent. Parents aren't faced with thirty other students to instruct or keep track of, nor must they follow a rigid schedule or curriculum geared toward passing a specific test. Grab the freedom to discover that education comes from involvement and not from inaction, not from students just sitting in a classroom.

# How To Not "Do School" At Home

*"It's absurd and anti-life to be part of a system that compels you to sit in confinement with people of exactly the same age and social class. That system effectively cuts you off from the immense diversity of life and the synergy of variety; indeed it cuts you off from your own past and future, sealing you in a continuous present much the same way television does..."– John Taylor Gatto*

In a normal brick and mortar classroom students usually sit at desks all day, while the blue sky creeps through the narrowed beige blinds of the classroom windows. Fully open blinds create distractions because birds are sitting perched in tree branches just barely within view. Students in a school classroom must feel like fish in a tank. Unable to escape from the small confined space of the desk, the bright blue of a warm September sky must beckon to them like the vastness of an ocean. On the chalkboard a teacher writes the day's lessons, barely aware that his or her students can hear the birds chirping in their heads and are daydreaming about the last bell ringing and running home to play in the remaining hours of sunlight.

I remember my mom telling me about one substitute teaching assignment she had in a classroom with no air conditioning, a dozen fans blowing from every corner of the room on a steaming hot day. She spent most of the class time yelling instructions left by the teacher over the roar of the fans. Would you pick this as a scene that would encourage learning? In most schools learning focuses more on behaving well, sitting still, standing in straight lines, tucking in one's shirt and, most of all, not talking. This highly restricted atmosphere might work for some children some of the time, but rarely for every child. Why shouldn't the educational environment reflect the individual's excitement, enthusiasm, and desire for hands-on activity, while also highlighting the student's abilities and strengths, minimizing and building success from weaknesses?

Many parents, having completed their mandatory schooling years in an institutionalized learning environment, might assume that the traditional classroom setting epitomizes the most effective way to learn for the majority of children. I mean, every school uses the same desk and chalkboard (or whiteboard) system, so it must work or else why do they keep it? So parents often jump right in and set up a classroom-like space where their child can learn at home. Sometimes they buy special desks and chairs and white, green or black boards. Some parents even buy globes and maps and other classroom "necessities" to simulate the look and feel of a public school classroom. These parents never question the model of their own schooling experiences, rarely pausing to observe how their children best absorb learning. Perhaps more parents should watch their children when they get a new video game, or a new toy, or a new doll. What do they do, where do they go, what propels them into engaging with this new activity? Most likely the child never chooses to sit at a desk to familiarize him or herself with this new object, nor do they usually elect to sit at a desk to study it.

Believing that one must replicate a school classroom at home can limit the success a home educated child might enjoy. Recreating the classroom sets up unnecessary boundaries around the child's imagination, interactions and potential learning experiences. If a parent thinks a child must sit at a desk, with books and a set curriculum, working on a set schedule, why not stay in school? Why take the leap into home education in the first place? If instead parents realized the limitations of the classroom, then their children could learn in whatever way best suits each child in each learning situation. The child might learn better, might retain more, and might find learning more interesting, more exciting and most of all, more fun.

Before children attended compulsory school, before the establishment of our mandatory public school system, children learned most things from direct observation, from hands-on experience with others in the community and the extended family. This sort of broad spectrum, firsthand education produced many great minds, leading to marvelous inventions and innovations, including some of the wonderful new and diverse learning resources available today. Like those found on the Internet, or those from excellent public libraries, public parks that offer great learning programs, nature centers, and dozens of unique museums that didn't exist a century ago, these resources are everywhere. Parents today can explore a wide variety of learning options, tailored to each child, richer and more diverse than ever before.

When I used to volunteer in our local Science and Natural History Museum I would observe school children when they visited. Mostly they spent their museum field trips following a very regimented schedule, standing in line and following instructions, rather than enjoying and exploring the exhibits. For most children the opportunity to spend time outside the classroom excited them, not particularly the idea of learning something while at the museum. When I was around home educating students who were visiting the museum they would be excited, too, but for different reasons, not in an attempt to escape their stagnant classrooms. I would watch these homeschoolers happily engaging in activities and interacting with the exhibits. They would ask questions, read the information on each exhibit, or ask their parents to read it for them. They were no longer simply passive observers, but they would participate in this learning journey and often made links between what they saw and what they had read, or seen in a movie, or watched on television, or had learned from other places they had visited. They were broadening their learning base and magnifying its impact in many different ways.

From my own experience I discovered that parents and children could arrange all kinds of field trips, based on the interests of individual students and families. Literally anything, any kind of trip or visit could turn into a fascinating learning experience once students were set free from the bonds of the classroom. Parents and children can arrange field trips based on student interests and the family's time and resources. Following a less traditional approach to education, the student can explore all kinds of learning. During unschooling "field trips" the student garners information that he or she might have otherwise missed in the rush to stay in line, to move on to the next scheduled activity, or to return to the school bus.

With home education, daily schedules can vary radically, adjusting to each family's specific needs. Learning from experiences, learning from doing, and learning according to one's own unique interests, the individual and family can create an educational environment that is much richer than any classroom. A walk in the woods, a few hours at the library, a day digging fossils, a trip to a historical site, can each trigger a series of cascading learning pursuits. Instead of spending money trying to replicate a classroom, spend time on uniquely interesting learning experiences, even if the student is sitting in a tree, or on the floor, or swinging in a hammock, reading a book, or perhaps just daydreaming.

When making the decision to home educate consider a more holistic and unstructured approach. Many books and online communities offer advice and information on how to successfully not "do school" at home. With help from these and other sources you can create an enriching learning environment that encourages self-expression, independence and intellectual thought and discussion. In my experience this learning environment creates a strongly self-motivated individual with a desire to learn. Giving the student an opportunity to independently study, to pursue self-directed learning, or unschooling, without a fixed curriculum, opens students to the skills necessary to achieve success later in life when thinking for oneself is essential.

When a student takes responsibility and decides to pursue a specific learning path, this choice empowers the student to work harder to fulfill personal goals and to achieve those goals. Enjoying the challenge of learning, writing and studying whatever interests the student, helps to uncover and develop whatever subjects each student finds most interesting. When and if the self-directed student decides to attend college, for example, the student might prefer enrolling in more challenging courses rather than engaging in lots of parties. Since the unschooling student has always enjoyed selecting specific learning goals and pursuing them, whether they are popular or not, he or she will be less likely to succumb to popular campus distractions.

I would never profess that one specific approach to learning will work for everyone. This approach might not be best for those children who are more comfortable in a formal school setting and who enjoy the particular social aspects of the public school environment. However, if a student struggles with the traditional school experience and is searching for an alternative, then unschooling just might be the answer. Just like searching for the best college, the best car value, the best price on groceries, search for the best form of education possible for each family member.

Not doing school at home can mean many things to different families. For me it meant volunteering at museums and historical events, reading about the French Revolution, involvement as president on a home school debate team, working part time at my local library to save money for a car, etc. I learned history and natural science hands-on through my volunteering activities. I read classic literature that I found while working at the public library. Even though I never took a formal test until the ACT, and though I never was in a traditional classroom from 5th grade on, I still attended college and completed my B.A. degree in four years.

Unschooling does not mean not being educated. Unschooling refers to learning in an informal, hands-on and actively engaged manner. Unschooled students don't follow a set curriculum or schedule and everyday involves opportunities to explore and learn new things. An unschooled student can spend weeks focused on a favorite subject, or spend a few hours each day reading and writing. Unschoolers can take seven straight weeks just to study algebra, or spend time studying to take the ACT or SAT, depending on his or her goals. Unschooled students can even study for and receive college credit by taking CLEP (College Level Examination Program) exams and earn dual credit for high school and college while completing compulsory attendance years.

There are no limitations or time tables. Families who are unschooling have more flexibility and advantages when making plans and choosing how to educate their children. Honestly, who doesn't want that? Schools use a set curriculum limiting what children are able to learn in each given day. In lower grades some schools even hand out tight little hour by hour, minute by minute schedules that teachers must follow. Public schools waste time in the classroom every day fulfilling the requirements set by the state, leaving little time for in-depth exploration of any subject. Instead children are taught topical facts to memorize, to ensure that each child can pass those mandated state exams. These exams are not used to educate the student, but instead to measure the effectiveness of how the schools educate children. Of course, this means that public school students only know how to do well on exams that cover an extremely limited amount of information, if they do well at all.

Why would you want to set the same limitations for yourself and your children outside of school? Choosing to unschool or home educate should be a decision based on wanting to create a better education, an education with more opportunities, better support, more diverse resources, and much more personal attention than a child might otherwise receive. Unschooling should be considered an alternative that intends to better prepare a child for success through exploring positive and limitless possibilities. Choosing to take a child out of compulsory attendance institutions, buying a desk, creating a classroom, and following a curriculum is really no different from having your child attend school. If "doing school" at home sounds appealing then why not leave education in the hands of those who consider themselves pros, who have earned degrees learning how to "do school."

Following the same structure of institutionalized school at home limits and isolates the student. This sort of instruction most likely comes to mind first when thinking of home education and leads people to believe that home educated students are not well socialized. Successful home educators are willing to relinquish the construct of the classroom ideal. Many people strongly believe in the importance and necessity of structure in education. I'll admit there are some children who absolutely need structure to function. Remember, unschooling and home education are simply an alternative and possibly not the best choice for every individual or family. But I do urge everyone to at least consider these options.

Consider what sort of educational approach might fit best. For my family the choice arose from what my parents believed were inferior educational facilities at the school I would have been attending. While a child I thought I would always attend public school. My dad worked third shift as a corrections officer and my mom ran a successful bed and breakfast, along with a bed and breakfast reservation service. We lived in a rural area with no children nearby. All of our family and friends lived a good distance away. If I wanted to sleep over at a friend's house my mom or dad drove about 45 minutes to an hour on mostly dirt roads out in the desert or mountain southwest. There were very few community activities for children during the day. My town had one very small museum, and an even smaller community center. But our library was great, several times larger than the community center.

Growing up with busy parents in a rural location, I attended school. I used to love the structure of the classroom. I would set up stuffed animals in a made-up classroom at home, with blocks for desks and crayons for #2 pencils. To me school felt completely normal. I understood the routine. I was an "A" student. I never felt the need to question attending school. For the most part I enjoyed learning new things and looked forward to school. I did however deal with my share of bullying and teasing from other students. That was probably the only source of discontent for me during my early years in school.

After moving to Ohio at the age of 10, my mother began to strongly question the nature and purpose of school and became my educational advocate. Distraught and discouraged by the sterile learning environment at the local district school I was required to attend, my mom questioned enrolling me. Both of us were put off by the appearance of the building itself. It looked more like an office, or worse, like the prison facilities where my father worked, with no interior walls, only corporate type space dividers, and no playground. I asked the principal giving us a tour of the facility why there wasn't a playground and received this reply: "Well, this IS an intermediate school." This response remains in my mom's memory because she believes that children should be allowed to be children and that children need a place to play, a playground. Any school that thought a playground was out of place for fifth graders probably lacked an understanding of what children require, how children learn most effectively.

I mean, come on, I know twenty-somethings who get excited about swinging on swings. Okay, even some thirty-somethings like to hang out on a playground now and then. I still get excited over swings, slides, having snowball fights, and jumping on trampolines.

That childhood sense of wonder and play never really disappears. At least it shouldn't. Life is short enough without people dictating the age limit on when you should stop playing on swings or sliding on slides. Seriously, what do they know? Are their kids perfectly adjusted? Do they even have kids? Why would you want to model yourself after such an absurd system? Sitting at a desk doesn't guarantee that a child will get anything more done than, say, if she or he sits outside under a tree, or on the couch, or curled up in a tent made from blankets and chairs. Every person has different needs that will either positively or negatively affect his or her ability to learn. I've been meaning to finish writing this very book for a couple of years now. Let me tell you, sitting at a desk for hours wasn't what motivated me. Instead it was just wanting to do it, to complete what I started. I believe the true indicator of whether one will be successful at home educating or unschooling comes down to a desire to learn. Trying to force the issue, making the home feel like a school, setting a strict schedule and following the protocol of institutional learning makes absolutely no sense for a family that elects to home educate. That sort of rigidity has yet to be proven as a successful teaching tool. Sure, it might expose a child to a certain amount of information, but if the child doesn't respond with genuine interest, are they really gaining an education?

Try to remember that it doesn't matter how much money you spend on the perfect set of books, classroom materials, or how well you organize the day, these things cannot guarantee a perfect student, teacher or approach to education. Home educating will bring laughter, fun, enjoyment and sometimes frustration into life. But emphasizing such things as trying to keep a child focused, quiet, paying attention, sitting still, and following instructions doesn't strengthen how well a student learns with home education. If that sort of discipline sounds like an appropriate way to get an education, then you should probably stop reading this book.

Instead of wasting all of that time trying to create the perfect replica of a school classroom you could enjoy learning together, with your child. Young children, even teenagers, don't learn better sitting still, because they don't always understand or want to listen. Each individual will relate to an activity in a different way. Sometimes he or she will instantly grasp the idea with a tangible fervor to learn. At other times he or she will respond poorly, struggle and find the subject too difficult, or that the student lacks interest. When students clam up, shut down, or get sassy parents need to consider that the student simply isn't interested. I know this from experience. I know that in the classroom setting rethinking and re-imagining the problems at hand takes more time than is usually available during a standard institutionalized school day. This often leaves those children frustrated and on their own, feeling less than competent, or worse, stupid. And all he or she probably needs is just a little extra support, or a little more time on his or her own, without any direct guidance. Sometimes a problem just has to wind its way through the brain, often following some very circuitous routes, before the student figures out a good solution, or maybe several good solutions.

Abandon the classroom model and get creative. All those fears, frustrations and anxieties of damaging a child are completely normal. Those feelings won't disappear when creating "school" at home. That will only complicate the entire process and lead to more frustration for everyone when things don't go exactly according to plan. Few know this, but in public schools many times things, including students, fall through the cracks. Schools start out with a "perfect plan," an intensely debated curriculum, a system of guidelines and a clear set of standards that takes an entire board of college educated people months to formalize. Even with all of that wasted time, money, and energy, often the teachers never get to complete that curriculum. Sometimes it takes longer than expected to go over one section of a book, or snow days interrupt the flow, or beautiful weather distracts the students. Maybe an influenza outbreak prevents a student, or many students, from taking scheduled exams, or test scores come back as unsatisfactory and students must repeat them. Students are really just guinea pigs in this whole imperfect system. I think if public education worked effectively then national test scores would be much higher. As a nation our students fall far behind on science and math scores, compared to the rest of the world, and especially compared to Asian countries that shamelessly outperform our students when it comes to standardized testing.

Public schools won't hesitate to pretend, persuade and convince you that schools are the best choice and often try to make parents feel inferior and unable to educate their own children. Why? One possible reason could be that if home educated children outperform institutionally educated students (which they do, on the whole), then public schools might have to admit that they are missing something, or perhaps doing something wrong. The institution of school does not foster the best and brightest. For that matter the best and brightest are most likely either attending private or parochial schools, or staying at home, being home educated, or lost somewhere in the drama, pressure, and bullying of the school environment.

Home educated students can leave the classroom behind, can learn in an environment free from the confines of a desk, a chalkboard, boring posters, bells ringing, bathroom passes, bullying, and constantly being shushed, told to stay quiet. Instead each can spend the day learning in an intuitive, interactive manner that truly fosters intellectual growth. The resources available to families today are mind-blowing. The Internet alone unrolls vast resources with opportunities for children to explore in-depth subjects that are far more intriguing and worthwhile than what they would generally pursue in a regular classroom while sitting at a desk.

Reading this book you might wonder about what gives me the authority or knowledge to suggest how children should be educated. I don't have much authority over anything. I can't even persuade my cats to stop kicking all the litter out of their litter boxes. However, I can relate my personal, firsthand knowledge, having elected to pursue unschooling and having learned through this type of holistic process. I've been through the struggles, fought the battles, faced the stress and the insecurities. I was there right from the start when my mother was dealing with this foreign concept of home education. When we started our journey as a home educating family we found few resources, little information or support for home educators, and even less for those families who wanted to explore unschooling.

To clarify, unschooling means not using any specific, or set curriculum. It is sometimes called child-directed learning, or child-motivated learning. That does not mean that unschoolers do not read, use textbooks, do not research, study, or educate themselves. We simply do not follow a specific plan laid out by a third party. Parents and children create the curriculum, if you must call it that, together. I personally refer to myself as a home educated student, because, well, I'm not really interested in explaining unschooling to every random person I meet. Though I do strongly believe in the merits of unschooling and I do intend to educate my own children in the same manner since I feel that the classroom experience is entirely outdated. So much information exists beyond the brick and mortar of the classroom, like the rich and vast learning resources and educational information online, plus lots of learning possibilities through great, free, local community activities, museums, children's programs, sports, and home school support groups. Even playhouses, theaters, and parks can share knowledge of language, biology, art and humanities. The idea of staying at home to learn something as a home educator comes from a misnomer, assuming that one should literally interpret the phrase "home education."

Experiencing life firsthand can teach more than any teacher in a classroom. No one learns to drive by sitting in a room watching someone else drive a car. Learning involves getting into the driver's seat and going somewhere, either physically or mentally, through imagination, thought, or hands-on interaction. If the mindset of the classroom offered the best materials for growth, then maybe you believe that all great breakthroughs in science, art, and music will occur in a classroom, as well. Newton witnessed and created some of his greatest scientific discoveries out of doors. Einstein (home educated) surely could not have done his many experiments in a classroom. No space exists in the classroom to explore a world full of possibilities. One needs much more room to make mistakes and/ or discoveries.

One must learn to be brave. I learned to take risks and I challenged convention. When I instruct children I realize how my experiences outside of any classroom changed me, made me a better teacher. I know that all the things I've learned are mostly things I would never have encountered in a classroom, at a desk, or while I was studying for an assessment test that didn't relate to anything in the real world. The real breathing, changing, innovating, creative world cannot be found or understood through an assessment test.

The classroom, the school-at-home idea, wears you out, locks you in, and makes you think that all the information needed comes in neatly structured perfect textbooks that someone else wrote. I would encourage parents and students to consider home education a viable choice that might fit into your life. And, if possible, you might even try unschooling. Remember to define and discuss goals and interests, like questioning about college, discovering if that's a goal, and then perhaps preparing for college courses at 14, or sometimes earlier, studying the anatomy of animals, learning to change the oil in a truck. Do whatever interests students; just get outside of the classroom trap.

# Home Education Beyond the Home

*"The aim (of education) must be the training of independently acting and thinking individuals who, however, can see in the service to the community their highest life achievement."- Albert Einstein*

Unschooled students thrive on turning a single day's activities into a month's worth of productive educational learning. If you are seeking the most effective learning path, then look no further. An unschooled student can not only absorb and retain more in less time than most institutionalized students, but also can connect and apply this learning to everyday, real world experiences. Many students especially appreciate the hands-on activities in which they often engage as an active segment of their learning protocol. The amount of information and experience an unschooled student can enjoy in a single day frequently surpasses the amount of information a publicly educated student might acquire in a week. Most of these experiences, by the way, probably won't transpire in the home, but somewhere out in the world, in real life.

Determined by a family's interests and needs, home educated children learn, grow and experience educational activities frequently and easily outside of the home. Home educating and unschooling families join support groups online, church groups, home-school co-ops, or through other online or local home education organizations. Within these groups families plan activities together and participate in events like: ice skating lessons, music lessons, science fairs, home school proms, book exchanges, chess clubs, swim parties, field trips, etc. Many home schooled and unschooled students enjoy traditional youth organizations like Girl Scouts, Boy Scouts, 4-H, the YMCA, and church groups, to name a few. With a little initiative and creativity families and home educated students participate in a multitude of social and educational events and activities. Unlike the traditional school setting, where parents remain on the sidelines, home educating parents play an active role through organizing, supervising, and/or instructing, always available during a variety of social opportunities with their children. Families get to know each other, and children grow up together through meeting up for visits to museums, or while attending classes in home school co-ops, or at camps, workshops, community events and presentations. All of these possible activities lure the unschooled student out of the house and into situations both educational and social. Maybe the unschooled student really likes snakes, for example. Then he or she can visit the zoo with the family, pick out books about snakes at the local library branch, and possibly participate in zoo programs offered on snakes.

Interested in fossils? An unschooled student could take a field trip to a natural history museum to learn more about fossils, possibly start a club with the help of his or her parents and notify other interested students through a home school group. Unschooled learners meet and make new friends while learning and interacting. Sounds just the same, if not better than what the socializing publicly schooled students claim to enjoy, right? But there is one big difference; most of the time, in most public schools, students are not talking and actively interacting with other students. They are being "shushed" and told to be quiet, the Golden Rule of the majority of public schools in this country. The unschooled learner, on the other hand, can talk, move, interact, get excited, be him or herself, expressing all the feelings and emotions that anyone might express when enjoying life and learning experiences.

Does an unschooled child really like a subject so much that books and field trips aren't satisfying enough? Why not immerse the student in an activity such as volunteering? Since home educated students aren't attending school during the day, they may volunteer at places like the zoo, nearby parks, museums, aquariums, historical villages, nature centers, etc. Plenty of not-for-profits, museums and theaters need volunteers. An unschooled student can either find existing programs or suggest that the facility start a program for home educated students. Because some programs will require parental participation, too, parents can enjoy the fun of learning new things right along with their students. Volunteering teaches students a great deal of responsibility. After a few weeks of training I began to give tours for school children through an 1812 cabin all by myself at a historical village near my home. My mom reminded me that in the 1800s children often performed the majority of jobs around the home and homestead.

I loved volunteering because I could socialize, both with other students and with a wide age range of visitors passing through the historical village or the museum. Also, I could dress up in lovely costume dresses from a specific historical period, dresses I often made myself, or I could discuss a wide variety of interesting topics with other volunteers and visitors. Even more, I greatly enjoyed the opportunity to educate others while gaining some amazing skills, like poise and self confidence when speaking in public. The ability to speak in front of a group of people can really define who you are and can help further your career as an adult. I can't tell you how grateful I am to volunteering for instilling in me the confidence necessary to speak in front of large groups. Trust me, when required to read a paper in a college class, or to train fellow employees at work, all my previous experience from volunteering really came in handy. At the time, I didn't realize that being in a fossil club or in 4-H would influence my adult life, but both opened many doors for me from an educational and social standpoint.

An unschooled student can explore a smorgasbord of community events: lectures, museums, concerts, dance recitals, theatrical performances, poetry readings, discussion groups, art and other exhibits. All of these amazing resources await the self-directed learner outside the realm of the traditional school setting. Public schools must follow very rigid schedules, state-mandated curricula, all frequently organized around mandatory testing. The need to elevate test scores perseveres, despite teacher and parent protests, as the primary goal of most public school systems. Students prepare constantly for assessments using many pretests, building up to the big annual state mandated test. Most schools offer student test scores as their proof that these approaches for educating students works effectively and correctly. Of course, more often than not, schools find that students are not meeting state expectations on these all-important tests.

Unschooled students don't waste much time with testing. The unschooled student's day might consist of various activities, such as: Lego robotics; gymnastics; interactive online learning courses; fencing; family activities, etc. Just ask an unschooling parent about free time while unschooling their child or children and they will laugh and tell you all about the hectic schedule they usually maintain. Unschooling children rarely spend all, or even much of their time at home learning. Parents drive their children to the park, or zoo, or museum, or nature center, and so forth, and then spend the entire day at these facilities supervising and monitoring these learning experiences with their children.

When unschooling you can pursue an endless list of possible classes, topics, subjects and ideas, while getting the unschooled learner out of the house and engaged in learning. Doing so requires passion, patience, creativity, energy, and a positive, open-minded attitude. One first step might involve joining a home school support group. Some groups adhere to narrower parameters than others, but you can choose the best group for your family, or join several groups, or even start a group yourself if nothing else fits. Families can network with other home educating families, ask lots of questions, record notes about interests and activities for future reference or consideration. Local events at museums, universities, theaters and parks usually offer free or inexpensive opportunities to get the unschooler out of the house. For example, many nature centers organize nature walks, special nature presentations, films, and day camps. Museums create programs specifically for a variety of ages, from toddler activities to overnights and volunteering opportunities, as well as trips to interesting and educational places. One of our local museums even offers older teens the chance to go to active archaeological dig sites and participate in the digs.

Unschooling families could even create their own nature walks or museum days by printing out bug or plant facts from the Internet and taking them along on a hike, or checking out library books on dinosaurs and then visiting a natural history museum, or watching a documentary on history and visiting a nearby history museum or historical site related to the documentary. For another active social aspect, parents could start groups with other families to go for hikes in the park or to watch educational films together, providing homemade popcorn and healthy snacks. Willingness to reach out to others, when needed, and to learn in a group setting creates many fun-filled learning experiences for everyone involved. Consider starting a club or group focused on a specific activity, like Frisbee golf or chess, and invite other home educating families to join. Remember the importance of parental involvement. Reading books together, discussing all the interesting things seen while visiting a goat dairy farm, or while at the nature center, or visiting an art museum, energizes children to learn more, stimulating great family dinner table conversations. So plan to engage, create and learn.

At the age of seventeen I worked three different jobs, saving money for my first car. I would search online car ads looking for an affordable vehicle. I kept records of how much money I was making, the sort of car I would like and what I would have to pay per month to afford it. I researched insurance rates, calculated gas costs per mile based on the average mileage the car could get, reviewed safety reports and customer satisfaction information. In the end I was the proud owner of a 5 speed Saab 900 S in gun metal gray, my very first car.

Confused? Let's try again. At the age of thirteen I greatly enjoyed walks in the park, visits to the nature center and studying about bugs and flowers. I would go exploring in the woods behind my house with my dad. In the creek bed we found huge broken up slabs of limestone jutting out everywhere, creating little waterfalls. Some slabs had broken down into small enough chunks to carry up to my front porch. Inside the chunks I found fossilized shells and squid-like forms. I didn't know at first what or how these shells occurred or what each was called, but I thought they were cool looking. My mom realized that what I had found could become a learning experience. What started as a collection of odd looking creatures stuck in rock evolved into getting a volunteer position at our local natural history museum, as well as starting a club for other young people interested in fossils, to get together and visit local parks and fossil rich sites to find fossils. That volunteer position then helped me get my first part time job working at the museum. With my interest in volunteering piqued, I volunteered at a historical village, which led to making friends with some really awesome adult volunteers. One of these adult volunteers suggested I attend a particular church with an excellent teen youth group and that led to meeting some of my best friends. Did I mention that all of these experiences arose from what happened in just one day while pursuing self-directed activities in home education? In that one day I learned about science, history, anatomy, chemistry, and, oh, yeah, had plenty of significant social experiences. My one day of discovering and learning was just like the day I spent researching buying a car, and both days are only two moments in all my years of daily activities while unschooling. Just a normal, average unschooling day can include multitudes of opportunities for exploring and growing into an intelligent, wise and well-balanced individual. How often can you say that about most average institutionalized school days?

Okay, now I'll be honest, this isn't your typical day. There were plenty of days when I just sat around and watched television, though I mostly watched PBS, since I was sort of addicted to the educational series "Nova" for awhile. Alright, I'll admit, I'm still addicted to "Nova," and now "Frontline." Okay, the truth, I did watch my share of crappy television too. I also fell into a simulated life computer game phase. Even so, I promise you that the amount of time I wasted pales by comparison to the amount of time wasted in the normal classroom. I've worked with students, tutoring them in school classrooms, and I know from experience that I often spend most of my time repeating myself and just trying to retain their attention. Whatever time is leftover I would spend reviewing, and maybe imparting some small nugget of information that the student might remember for the next five minutes. Don't get me wrong, I adore working with children. Realistically though, most children and adults have a difficult time focusing when other more interesting things are going on, even something as simple and distracting as another person fidgeting and squirming in the desk nearby.

Lacking adequate mental stimulation, either while in school or at home, easily distracted students face punishment for disrupting class and not focusing. To spend every foreseeable future weekday sitting still and staying quiet would truly depress me. Vying for attention and fidgeting in a crowded classroom while a teacher shushes and criticizes students for simply behaving like normal bored children sounds demoralizing. Each day of my home education I focused on many different subjects, allowing little opportunity for boredom. So everyday I could discover different things. One day I went on a trip to the Air Force Museum. Let me just say that if my family could have afforded to pay for flying

74

lessons, I would have been a pilot in a heartbeat. My mom found books about Amelia Earhart for me after that trip. Later I flew in a small plane as part of an Aircraft Owners and Pilots Association free flight program for young people. Today they offer a similar program that is known as the AV8RS program. That really sold me on flying and I had many daydreams about what it might have been like for Amelia Earhart.

During many sweltering afternoons at county or state Fairgrounds, I modeled clothing that I'd designed and sewn myself at 4-H fairs and division competitions. At these events I learned the importance of sportsmanship, air conditioning and individual expression. I learned how to form my own thoughts and opinions based on my interests. I could spend an entire day reading about the French Revolution (I did; I know it's nerdy). Maybe some children could really care less about my explorations into how our founding fathers wrote the Declaration of Independence in 1777. But, maybe, just maybe, some might find it interesting.

The average home schooled kid doesn't come home tired and cranky from boredom, or frustrated and upset from peer pressure or bullying, nor does he or she face a huge pile of homework. If a home educated student did face all those issues, I could completely understand not caring about some old dead guys, or a bunch of rocks in the backyard. Instead my parents took an active interest in my learning, taking part in my explorations, because, of course, they enjoyed learning, too. This shared knowledge gave us something to talk about at the end of the day when we sat together for dinner. I really enjoyed those moments. I enjoyed everyday of my self-directed home education experience.

I could continue to pursue my love for competitive figure skating while I learned about topics and subjects that interested me. I could read books considered way above my "grade level," because, well, I could. No one chose specific books for me to read, or imposed restrictive rules or standards on me. If I wanted to sew a dress, paint a painting, hike around the woods taking photos, go out to laser tag with friends, I did (with parental permission, of course). I didn't worry about homework. I didn't stress about tests or exams. Each day was completely up to me, with the support and guidance of my mother. Dad was usually at work, but when he was at home, he often participated, too. I ensured the success of my own education, and let me tell you, having that responsibility taught me a great deal about consequences and decision making.

If you think about it, kids in school aren't given much responsibility. They're in school from the age of five or six until eighteen, or until twenty-two if they then go on to college. During that period of time someone tells them what to study, where to go, when to do this and how to do that, leaving no space for the development of personal thoughts, learning moral values and/or mastering how to assume responsibility for themselves and their personal decisions. My everyday life was my personal responsibility. I decided whether I woke up at 8:00 a.m. or 1:00 p.m.

When I was a teen my hormones really messed up my sleep pattern. Usually my day started around 10 a.m. If there were activities scheduled that day for me to attend, things that I wanted to attend, that's what I did. Sometimes my family would go to museums, visit parks, hosting other home schoolers at our house for many different learning experiences. I also had volunteer shifts, and sometimes a part-time job. On a typical day I would read, watch television, spend time discussing various topics with my mom, hang out with friends, and take care of my cat. At the end of the day sometimes I would feel like I had accomplished something and sometimes I wouldn't. No one ever told me what to think or told me what I had to know. In that way my typical day was not typical at all. Whatever I did or thought was completely at my own discretion. What a great deal of responsibility to have as a young person!

I chose my everyday activities and I look back on those eight years of homeschooling with pride. I decided to become a volunteer.

Since I learned hands-on about history, as an adult I feel a deep attachment to my country and to other people. Through my everyday experiences I learned skills that I never expected would become useful in my future. For example, at the age of fourteen I taught other children about the history of the 1800s. I volunteered my time while creating learning opportunities for other students. From those days I spent in a period-appropriate dress that I had sewn myself, interpreting historical buildings for visiting students and families, I learned the importance of integrity, patience, and how to contribute to others.

During my pre-teen years I volunteered at our wonderful local Science and Natural History Museum, learning about anatomy and natural science. When volunteering I instructed children on how the digestive system functioned, or I helped visitors exchange their own fossil finds for different ones in the museum's Trading Post. I made friends during my volunteer shifts and connected with other museum staff. After a couple of years of volunteer work I applied for a paid position in the gift shop. My days spent in the Natural History Museum taught me a great deal about science and then led me to getting my first paycheck. Each day brought with it new possibilities to acquire more knowledge. From learning about the structure of the human lung to providing customer service, each unschooling day came with a different set of challenges and opportunities for growth.

At the age of 17, I divided my time between two different part-time jobs, saving some money for college and to buy my first used car. I also took driver's education at my local high school and studied for my driver's test. Some days I sat cheering in the bleachers at high school track meets in which my boyfriend ran. On weekends my friends and I went to school dances, proms, formal dances, and homecomings. We went to movies and parties at the homes of other friends. Typically though, during the day, when not working or socializing, I read books on history, art and/or design, played piano and ice skated. I worked hard to earn money for the things I needed, like a new computer and a new piano. Although some days included hours of reading and academic work, plenty of days did not.

Once I decided I wanted to attend college, I studied for and took both the ACT and SAT exams. Suddenly I spent most of my days focused on studying for college entrance exams, and visiting colleges that I might attend. Focusing each day on obtaining the skills needed for a successful four years at college, my unschooling experience became more academic and organized. Unlike earlier, when I could play more and divide my time among many interests, I realized that if I wanted to go to college I would need to do whatever they required of me, to fulfill all the entrance requirements, some of which are different for home educated students. For example, I had to help prepare transcripts because I didn't have a school counselor whose job it was to do this. I had to research and discover exactly what each college expected from me before applying for admission, since each one might require different documents to substantiate my pre-college years of learning. And I had to find full-tuition scholarships, too, since I could not afford to go to college any other way.

Beginning my first year of college was both a terrifying and enlightening phase in my life. I hadn't attended an academic class in about nine years, though I had attended lectures and talks at universities and colleges from time to time. And I had attended a wonderful "Explore-A-College" program one summer that I had loved, with intense classes and many hours spent in the college's ceramics studio learning about raku pottery. But still, walking into my first college class, Intro to Drawing, I panicked a bit at the prospect of not knowing what to do. I failed to realize that everyone else in the studio was feeling the same way. After my first day of classes I relaxed, realizing that despite my unschooled background I clearly understood the requirements of college and knew I could succeed. In my freshman year I received the award for academic excellence on my campus. One of my art professors had surprisingly recommended me for the award. Both the award and my grades reassured me that unschoolers are indeed intelligent and capable of doing very well on college level work. Over the course of my freshman year I achieved higher grades than fellow students while I consistently and punctually attended my classes, unlike many of my peers. Most struggled to turn in projects, to arrive on time, and quite a few failed to finish many classes. Though I didn't attend or graduate from a traditional public school, each day while an undergraduate demonstrated that an unschooler can survive and succeed, despite the stresses and academic rigors of college. I feel that the days I spent in college clearly showed that educational achievement can readily follow a unique and unusual learning path.

I found that the most important aspect of the typical home school day came from spending time with my family. Perhaps this is because the most critical contributions to a child's success are contributions from people who support them, and not necessarily just the support from parents. Often very successful people thank a mentor from college, or a teacher from their school for giving them the support they needed to succeed. Personally I don't see why the mentor and teacher just as easily and naturally can't be the parent. Family involvement in the day-to-day activities of home educated children is often a critical element in their success.

To help you understand my daily routine as an unschooled home educated student I've listed some of my example activities:

**- Attending concerts, live performances, and plays:**

As a home educated student I could read about Shakespeare and attend local performances of the bard's plays. Sometimes just reading and discussing the plays with other home schoolers can stimulate other wonderful learning opportunities. Another activity I enjoyed was learning about classical music, studying the lives and music of Mozart, Beethoven, and many other composers, and then attending concerts, many of which are available for free through universities and music conservatories in many communities. Afterwards I could spend some of my time learning to play a classical instrument, learning to read music, write music, study music theory. In many communities students can find free performances from community orchestras, to local music schools and performing arts high schools. I often attended plays at local theaters or in park presentations, and then enjoyed discussing how the play was written, the plot, the characters, or meaning of the play with my mom or with other home schoolers who attended the same play. Then I could go home and write and perform a play of my own. These activities helped me develop language art skills, music comprehension, history, and much more.

**- Visiting museums or historical sites:**

Since my dad worked at a huge museum facility I often visited the Science and Natural History Museum, the History Museum, or the Children's Museum there. My mom also took me to the Art Museum or our local Contemporary Art Center. When we traveled I visited all kinds of different museums, reading everything at each museum. We'd check web sites for scheduled special events or simply would plan a visit with bag lunches and plenty of time to learn. One of the biggest advantages of home schooling is that one can spend as much time as one wants in each section of a museum, without being rushed to stick to a preordained school schedule and bus ride back to the school. One can study fossils in natural history and learn how archaeologists sift through packed mud for tiny bones and creatures, long ago cemented in rock. Since one of the day care facilities I had occasionally attended when I was very young was run by an archaeologist who would take us to nearby dig sites in New

Mexico, I had fond memories of these types of studies. One could learn about history through museums or visiting historical sites or villages, all of which schedule seasonal and special events. These events often include historical interpreters who have studied a particular period and can share further insights and information about the past.

At children's museums home educated students can learn about many different subjects, like science, history, geography, and astronomy. The list is endless. Art museums can also offer insight into history, composition, color concepts, gestalt theory, design, and chemistry. Both ceramics and painting are deeply rooted in the science that creates the pigments, as well as studying the surface designs that make them beautiful. I recall how much I enjoyed learning about the chemistry of creating ceramic glazes and the complexities of mixing colors. One can develop skills and knowledge in science, art, engineering, chemistry, history and much more. Asking questions taught me how airplanes fly and how some paintings last for centuries.

**- Visiting the Public Library:**

Like museums, libraries often have special events scheduled for both children and adults. One can usually check out the library website to find out more about these events. One could also just go and spend a day at the library, perusing the collections, searching for something interesting. I would often read, graze, select a stack of interesting books and periodicals, and enjoy flipping through the pages. I also found book clubs and other activity clubs at my local library, like an Anime club, a drama club, even a knitting club. And I also created clubs with other home educating families. I could pick a theme or subject to study for a day, a week, a month, or a whole school year. And I loved checking out more books than I could ever possibly read. Warning: just remember where you put them all because fines can get costly. I immensely enjoyed spending time at our local libraries; they are such amazing community assets. In fact, I spent so much time at my local branch library that I ended up working there as a student assistant, which was another learning experience.

**- Attending lectures:**

Home educated and unschooled students can attend lectures at art museums, colleges, universities, libraries, community government activities, parks, coffee houses, and many special events. The majority of such lectures are free, including loads of free online lectures with Internet resources today. Going to lectures opens new doors, brings in new information, and is a great activity and yet another opportunity to learn.

**- Create playgroups:**

Just like publicly educated students, home educating and unschooling students can organize their own play or social groups. The primary difference between these and other groups might be that home educating families usually organize groups around educational activities, like trips to the zoo, museum, or park, in their play group meetings. Playgroups build social skills while children engage in a wide variety of learning activities.

**- Organizing activities around specific interests:**

Want an easy way to get a home educated or unschooling student out of the house? Find an activity that would interest the student and then go pro-active. Contact other family members and friends, tell them about this interest and see what sort of activities you can plan. When I was a young person my father was really interested in history, the Civil War in particular and slavery, to be specific. So, of course, I became interested, too. My mom did some research and found out that there were a number of Underground Railroad sites in our area along and on both sides of the Ohio River. After some planning my mother organized and announced a mini field trip open to any other interested home educating families to visit these sites on one particular day. The catch to this tour was that the historical interpreters for all these sites were only available for a group our size on one particular Sunday. That Sunday just happened to be Super Bowl Sunday. But my mom went ahead and arranged this private group tour, not sure how many would show up. Imagine her surprise when a total of 80 people followed through, with kids and whole families, wending their way along the Ohio River in a long line of minivans to see these fascinating sites and to listen to what the historical interpreters presented for us. This was an amazing experience and one that a student could never arrange while attending a public school. Even my mom had never imagined that so many parents would opt to spend their Super Bowl Sunday visiting Underground Railroad sites rather than watching football, but that's how involved parents of home educated students often become. Organizing such an activity might seem daunting, but all it takes is a little online research and a few phone calls. Then announce it to the group and see how many show up.

## - Visiting parks:

Going to the park opens the great world of the outdoors to students who play and learn at the same time, while enjoying this affordable learning activity. Families can transport their own field guide books about bugs, plants, birds, fossils, etc., to parks, while dreaming up a scavenger hunt or natural science study. This and many other activities can involve the entire family, all ages. What better way to bond with each other and learn? Parks also often offer classes, lectures and other educational activities throughout the year. Nature walks in the fall can help students learn about the seasons, or provide an opportunity to collect fallen leaves and learn to identify them. Check your local park calendars for special activities all year-round and enjoy the fine work that the naturalists and volunteers organize for anyone who wants to participate. One of our favorites each year was to visit a nearby State Park during maple sugaring season where we watched and learned about how they tap the trees, collect the liquid, boil it up in big vats and transform it into delicious maple syrup. The highlight for us was the wonderful pancake breakfast the park offered at very reasonable cost, served with their homemade maple syrup.

**- Taking Classes:**

Probably the most obvious way to get home educated students out of the house would be by enrolling in various classes in the community. I know that may sound like an oxymoron, home educated students taking classes, but sometimes students will enjoy learning in a different environment with a specific teacher. No need to always reinvent the wheel when plenty of highly qualified people offer classes on many subjects. Parents do not have to handle everything themselves. Just like public schools, the home educating parent doesn't always feel qualified to teach every subject that students want to study. Taking some classes can introduce the home educated student to other voices, other methods, other interesting people, and a chance to involve themselves in something separate from the rest of the family. Such activities build independence and better social skills. Recently I've noticed that more and more places have been offering classes specifically for home educating families during the day when public school students are in school and can't attend. Many home educated students set up piano, guitar, or other musical instrument classes or lessons during the day, too. Often students can find excellent art classes during the day. Home educated students can also enroll in summer classes and camps at parks, aquariums, zoos and museums to study many different subjects, like natural science, biology, and art history for a few examples. Classes can expand the home educated student's knowledge and involve students with new social groups and new opportunities for both learning and socializing.

## - Playing Sports:

Home education and unschooling does not limit one's ability to be active and play sports. Playing a sport builds discipline, patience, focus, strength and teamwork, all of which are important steps toward maturity and adulthood.  I spent eight years involved in competitive figure skating and the skills I learned helped me develop into a stronger, healthier and more disciplined adult.  Involvement in any sport requires a desire to learn the skills necessary to be good at the game, or whatever challenges one faces while participating. Parents can help cultivate the learning of new skills by helping students research to select the right sports involvement for his or her particular abilities.  Playing sports can instill that desire to face challenges and to conquer even difficult things. Sports also offer the home educating student the opportunity to bond with others, creating new friendships through this type of active involvement.

I've known home educated students involved in many different sports:  tennis, golf, archery, fencing, Tae Kwan Do and other martial arts disciplines, figure skating, hockey, skiing, snowboarding, equestrian training, rock climbing, bicycling, riflery, canoeing, kayaking, swimming, diving, just to name a few.  And most communities offer a wide variety of team sports through their community and intramural recreation programs.  From baseball to soccer, from basketball to football, from tennis to cricket, just about any student can find a sport that fits him or her perfectly.  And if students want to pursue something that isn't already available, just find someone who is involved in this sport and propose that they offer classes or private lessons. Not attending school does not exclude students from all those "normal" things publicly schooled students enjoy, such as playing sports or going on field trips. Opportunities for learning activities exist everywhere, sometimes in very surprising places. Even flying a kite can be a learning activity in which one can learn about physics and aerodynamics. And knitting a sweater involves quite a bit of math, especially geometry, and helps with hand and eye coordination. In my chapter "How to Find Excellent Learning Resources," I write about how one can find materials to accompany activities, or to create activities. On the next page you can create a variety of your own possible learning activities.

| **Interests** | **Place** | **Activity** |
|---|---|---|
| Example: Fossils | Natural History Museum | Read books about fossils |

_____

_____

_____

_____

_____

_____

_____

_____

_____

_____

_____

_____

_____

_____

_____

_____

_____

_____

# Finding Excellent Learning Resources

*"I don't think we'll get rid of schools any time soon, certainly not in my lifetime, but if we're going to change what's rapidly becoming a disaster of ignorance, we need to realize that the school institution 'schools' very well, though it does not 'educate'; that's inherent in the design of the thing. It's not the fault of bad teachers or too little money spent. It's just impossible for education and schooling ever to be the same thing."*– John Taylor Gatto

Accessing a large pool of resources gives home educators a huge advantage because outside of the classroom walls learning possibilities far exceed those available within the classroom setting. Finding amazing learning resources involves taking a very proactive role in education. If I wanted to learn more about a specific topic my mom would tell me to go look it up online, or would take me to the library to read books on the subject. Going one step further, we often discovered youth volunteer opportunities rich in educational resources. One of those youth volunteer positions I enjoyed was at our local Museum Center. While volunteering there I had access to thick binders full of facts and fellow volunteers and employees eager to share a great deal of personal insight and information.

Many volunteer organizations provide binders and books as part of their training programs, or online research tools so that volunteers are well read and informed. What an excellent resource for the home educated student! First of all, getting out of the house and serving the community, and secondly, those staff members involved with these sorts of programs who have access to and are usually more than happy to share the resources they have on the subject.  One might not believe this, but kids really can learn a great deal from interacting and asking questions of these adult mentors beside whom they are volunteering.  Remember the importance of doing your research and fully vetting any youth volunteer program to insure your child's safety.  Here is where close parental involvement and supervision can really pay off.  A predator would find most home educated students to be less than opportune targets because they almost always are with one or both parents.

Another way to discover more interactive resources involves going to local libraries. Many offer free educational events and lectures.  Some even get authors of books to come and speak, another great way to get engaged in interesting discussions.  This also goes for local coffee shops, theaters, music halls, and art museums.  All of these places are overflowing with helpful resources and offer programs for children and adults.  Keep in mind the more interactive or engaging the learning resource the better the experience, though sometimes one might prefer using books to supplement an unschooling education.  Try not to get locked into a set of textbooks, since these are often expensive and go out of date quickly.

Instead try looking for information on a particular subject through a search engine or online library catalog.  Online library catalogs offer a quick and easy way to find a diverse collection of books.  An online search on a topic offers a seemingly endless array of websites full of information as well.  Another way to find a breadth of possible books to read would be through Google books, where one can search for a subject just like one would with a library catalog.  However Google books offers a broader choice of books to explore, since they aren't limited by a library's collection space.  Some of the books are free to read, while others only offer limited previews.  Despite that you can browse through fascinating books, then possibly find those books at your local library or an online book store.

I used this technique when choosing books for my last two years of college. I could type in a few keywords. For example: "Art in Story." This search brought up a wide array of books both on art and story, and books that discuss both of the subjects. Once I found books that appeared to apply best, I would search specifically for that book in my local library catalog. Most of the time I could locate the books I wanted for free from my local library. However, I did have to buy a few. Easily browsing such a wide selection of books online helped me a great deal while in college. Often locating resources you need can frustrate students, so don't simply rely on the library, and don't simply rely on a set curriculum. If you want a fully rounded education then following a set of books with a particular order or guideline won't necessarily work. Why limit learning, with so many books offering varying perspectives available?

Often you can learn the most by comparing the perspectives and/or approaches of different books, authors, and different websites. In my experience, when I used a wider range of resources I was able to better comprehend the subject I was learning. The ability to learn in this manner became a huge asset while I was attending college. Knowing how to find other resources, apart from the assigned textbooks, supplements an education and makes for a more complete understanding of a subject. Knowing how and where to find a wide variety of resources will greatly benefit one for all future research projects, college exams, and for job opportunities.

I found that focusing on a few keywords of interest can provide better results and yield more interesting books. For example, if I was searching for biology information, you can imagine how many thousands of pages of information would turn up on a search engine. Instead consider what specifically interests you. But if you have no idea, then by all means go for the mass information search and dive right in; eventually one aspect or branch of that subject will pique your interest. Don't worry about whether something should be learned, or needs to be learned. In home education there is no such thing as "need to know."

Explore the possible resources and multitudes of subjects. Parents should consider what sort of resources will get the best reception and response from the child, and if you are a student, think about future goals and current interests when choosing how and what to learn. Will reading a website on the subject be adequate? Should you go to the library or a bookstore? What about attending a lecture? What about using worksheets or interactive software? There are so many excellent resources available. By using search engines, libraries, community centers, even college websites, you can easily discover what will work best. It might take some time to find the right resources. Luckily though, the Internet has made it immensely easy to do this. Make sure to take advantage of what you can find on the Internet.

Nowadays everyone and their dog has some sort of IT connection: website, twitter, flicker, blog thing, or something else in which information and resources are posting at a record pace. Blogs are an awesome way to learn from others who share their interesting and creative experiences. Many home educating parents have personal blog sites in which they share the good, the bad and the ugly of home education. I searched for homeschooling parent blogs through the yahoo search engine and many websites that offer resources and support came up. Many college professors and teachers have blog sites, too. There are science blogs, music blogs, writing blogs, etc, all of which offer some great insight and different perspectives, and all of which will share a wealth of information, most of the time for free. The benefit of blogs are the posts, links, and websites sharing even more information on specific subjects.

Don't like blogs? Then check out what the local natural history museum or children's museum lists on their website. Many museum sites link to excellent online resources, while also promoting their own events, as I mentioned above. Even social websites can be useful in finding resources since nearly every Internet inclined business has some sort of social media page. These pages may seem silly to some, however, they can have links to resources about lectures, books or information. One of my favorites at the moment would be the CAC (Contemporary Art Center) in Cincinnati. By liking the CAC on a social site I can quickly be informed about upcoming lectures, exhibits and events. Since I'm on my online social page frequently this works as a great resource for me. I've found that social networking pages are updated more often and make it easier to find dates and information, like special events, overnights, and volunteer opportunities.

Honestly, social network websites aren't for everyone. No worries though, you can still find whatever you want to investigate more on official websites. Want to explore more about history? Check online for any historical sites nearby. Not only will you locate some interesting places to go, but you will also create a hands-on experience for the unschooling student. Visually engaging in an activity tends to make it more memorable. Instead of simply saying," Oh, hey, I read a book on that once," the unschooling student can instead say, "Hey, remember that time we visited the historical village and I learned how Civil War soldiers only had hardtack to eat?" That's something I learned volunteering at our park's historical village. Getting engaged in something that requires hands-on involvement ranks as one of the best ways to learn.

Probably the most important thing to realize about learning resources in the world of unschooling is that they can extend well beyond simple paper and pencils. Instead of using a book as a reference in a classroom, the unschooled student can create a whole experience. Remembering an activity requires less effort than recalling details from a book. When you combine the activity with the book resource you significantly increase the odds of learning and retaining something new. If the unschooling student enjoys reading a book about geology, then combine that reading with a film, or going to a natural history museum or exhibit to learn more.  Also, there are many online videos and resources through PBS, and, yes, even Youtube, that can assist students who want to visually explore a subject even further.

Surprisingly, Youtube.com hosts a plethora of informative and instructional videos.  Though that might sound a little frightening, many educational videos coexist with some of the sketchier ones.  I recommend adult supervision for young children when it comes to Youtube.com.  If unsure about Youtube, then first check out the awesome lecture series TED (Technology, Entertainment, Design), because TED always amazes me.  Probably one of the best online video lecture resources on the web (also, available through streaming players like Roku and Apple TV), TED features lectures with some of the most brilliant minds of our time.  I would strongly encourage an unschooling student to check out TED and learn from featured professionals in the fields of science, art, music, poetry, design, politics, technology, etc.  TED is truly a great resource and one that can't be found in most traditional classrooms.

Another great source, iTunes, presents podcasts, along with courses available on iTunesU, which they update constantly.  iTunes podcasts are free and are like spoken blog pages that cover the gamut from language, to travel, to music, to art, and can be synchronized to an ipod or ipad.  Students can play these in the car on trips or while working on other projects.  Talk about an easy and affordable resource.  iTunes U also offers free audio courses, such as a Stanford University course on the anatomy of the heart, or the Asian Art Museum's course on the arts of Japan.  Students can find audio courses on economics, physics, ancient Greece, and a wide assortment of foreign language courses.  Did I mention that all of these are free?  These only require a free iTunes account.

Some resources may require a little more advanced computer skills, but, trust me, anyone can learn.  And some courses might at first look too difficult.  Try them anyway.  Who has determined whether an eight year old can read about physics or about building a car engine? I was reading <u>Les Miserables</u> at the age of 15. Not familiar with that book? Let me start by saying it's almost three inches thick and set in 1815-1832 in revolutionary France. Granted, I might have been a strange child. Despite that my parents were often surprised at what I would select to read and learn. For my mom finding the resources to foster my interests was a learning experience she enjoyed and that really brought us closer together. So, don't worry about how well a child will comprehend something; think about what the child wants to learn.

Don't underestimate the usefulness of pulling information from a variety of resources. Don't feel intimidated about whether or not you are finding the right resources. Just keep exploring and you will find whatever you need, eventually. You will soon grasp how successful a particular resource is by whether or not the unschooling student is understanding enough to discuss what he or she is learning. If not, then try again. Look for other resources. Try different sensory approaches by listening to something, or watching videos online. Sometimes locating just the right resources might require looking in unexpected places, too. Don't have access to the Internet at your home? Wi-fi networks are popping up everywhere, often available for free. Most public libraries also provide computers that patrons can access. Talk about killing two birds with one stone; once the time on the computer runs out students can browse the book shelves for even more information. When I was a teen I used to check out huge stacks of books on our library systems "educator" card which offered unlimited access to most library resources. I did not always have the time to read through every book, but I certainly developed a love for books. I still would list books as my favorite resource. As an artist my resources are art books full of beautiful photos of artwork and anatomy books with details of the human body that I love to draw. I also especially enjoy books on art theory and creativity.

When I first started my unschooling journey such amazing resources as iTunesU and TED did not exist. Even with the somewhat limited resources available then, I could still find all the information I needed to be successful. Taking the time to look for resources matters most. So, constantly remain on the lookout. One can find excellent resources in something as simple as a packet of seeds to plant in a garden. Do you recognize how much science a student can learn while growing a small garden? Check out the gardening section in your library and explore for yourself. Many small things can serve as resources for education. Look for those "little" opportunities. Do you have fabric sitting around? Maybe a pattern for a craft? Do you have knitting needles or a sewing machine? Have you explored 4-H? With unschooling students can explore the educational potential of things that they might have otherwise overlooked in a traditional school. The unschooling student can turn almost anything into a learning experience. Even trips to the grocery store can fulfill many different learning opportunities. For example, an unschooled student can calculate the sale price of an item, or learn how to find the lowest price based on the cost per unit, usually posted on the grocery store shelf. In a flash, any trip to almost any store can easily turn into a series of math lessons.

In the following section I'll explain how my mom started her own support group in the summer of 2000. Her support group functions completely online, for free, and fosters inclusion of all home school families, offering support and important information to more than1000 home educated families in our metropolitan area.

**Form Your Own Support Group**

Thanks in part to the Internet, home educating families can easily network, blog, share and organize activities and interact with each other. Many home educating and unschooling parents maintain their own blog sites that chronicle their alternative education journeys. Through online blogs individuals can connect and share, and create their own support groups. Beyond blogs, home educators can join many online "groups" for free. Some of these "groups" can be found on yahoo.com, google.com, as well as meetup.com.

Any parent or home educated student can create his or her own home education group with these websites, or through a blog site. Such groups encourage families to share information about upcoming activities, events, or resources. Online support groups are also a great place to ask questions about home education and unschooling, about local laws and regulations, often eliciting a variety of responses from others in the group. When one begins to learn about home education, asking questions and getting answers from other home educating or unschooling families can serve as a lifeline. Online archived group posts allow newcomers to search for posts on specific topics or subjects and can open many doors for those just beginning to explore home education.

When my mother elected to exercise her right to educate me at home she could find few resources that were inclusive enough and that focused on unschooling and other unstructured learning options. At the time only one established home school organization existed that claimed to be inclusive, or not based on a specific set of religious principles. After a couple of years, disillusioned and disappointed by the politics of this group, my mom decided to create her own free online support group, open to all families without any curricular prejudice or religious affiliation bias. My mom's group, with more than 1000 member families, is a very active group based on my mom's desire to create a positive, open, and informative group for all home educating and unschooling families. Since her group began it has fielded over 40,000 posts from members about topics that range from upcoming events, activities, and play-dates, to members selling their used home schooling materials, to answering questions about requirements of our state home education regulations. Members regularly share interesting resources and, most importantly, this group has connected families and allowed them to form a community of mutual interest, a point of connection for all those who venture into the wonderful world of home education.

After more than a decade of dedication and thousands of unpaid hours spent monitoring, posting, facilitating and sharing information on her online group site, my mom will soon begin her own subscription blog site. When she started this group she had no idea how large and popular it would become. Home education, as an alternative, has grown immensely popular over the last decade. The resources available today far surpass what we found when I started my unschooling journey. For that matter, those who undertake home education or unschooling today will find much more support and be far better prepared for this journey. Students who enter the world of unschooling can resource and learn a great deal more than I did. Access to information has increased considerably and should continue to expand over the coming years, as more become available online, with the vast majority available totally for free.

If being responsible for an entire online community group doesn't appeal to you, don't worry. You can simply join a number of free online groups and soak up the information that members share. Don't feel obligated to post messages or get heavily involved in discussions. But feel free to introduce yourself, to ask questions and find out about the various approaches to home education. You can arrange play dates with other families with similar interests, or simply read posts about upcoming events and decide which ones fit your family's interests. Similar online groups exist in nearly every city across this country. Join more than one if you can, to find out how other families are spending their time, organizing their studies, and where they find their resources. One can also search online and find out if there are any home school organizations in your area that hold regular meetings or events, if the online community doesn't appeal to you. Find whatever sort of group, community, or support fits your family, your lifestyle, but make sure to get involved. Home education will never be a spectator sport. To realize the most success, one must be pro-active, take responsibility for and participate in all aspects of this family friendly learning adventure.

One of the great pleasures of home education and unschooling is meeting and supporting the community of other home educators, while enjoying similar support from other families. Home education and unschooling make many people imagine learning situations that isolate children at home, like some kind of cult. In today's homeschool world one can find so many activities in which to participate, all arranged, advertised and planned by other families, that a home educating individual might spend very little time at home. One example of this was a family with two young boys who were members of my mom's group. While a young teen I offered to babysit for home education families and would babysit the two boys often. Their mother would always comment to me about how busy her children were with sports, or clubs, or science classes. I remember thinking that she seemed so much more involved and busy with her children than the mothers of my public school friends. This was the same way with my mom.

Through various online support groups and homeschool organizations home educating parents I've met can participate in a dizzying array of activities. Many of these children, some of whom I've taught myself, are constantly going from one thing to another. Many parents have commented to me how much they appreciate their online groups for providing them with all the great activities and resources for their children. Becoming part of a group, even if only through your Internet server connection, will greatly benefit any home educating student or family.

One of the biggest differences between the PTA and the home education community is 24/7 accessibility. The home education community doesn't limit access to a set schedule, so families and students can contact each other in a multitude of ways, whenever and wherever appropriate. To arrange get togethers and field trips one can post messages to a homeschool e-group, a social networking site, transmit a quick email, twitter or send a text message. One need not wait until a scheduled, official business meeting to ask questions or raise concerns. Since many of the new home educator's questions have been answered multiple times in these types of groups, often a group moderator, or another member, will simply refer the member to specific group archived posts or files for answers, all readily accessible online to members.

So why would you want to start your own group if all these other groups already exist? Because you could more easily connect with home educators who live in your part of town. You could find those who live in your rural area, locate those who might subscribe to a specific educational philosophy, or you might want to meet up with those who have children in a certain age group, like pre-kindergarten age, or early elementary, junior high, or high school-aged students. Perhaps you prefer finding some who are actively pursuing specific activities, like music, art, sports, science, or even those who follow your same religious preferences. Many of the original home education groups organized around religious principles. Today one can find so many other options, much broader, more inclusive groups that sample a cornucopia of resources. A group could organize around unique learning options that a homeschooling family might locate in a specific area. Best that one not wall oneself in too tightly in today's wonderful and diverse world of home education.

Sometimes families hope to address certain learning problems they face with students who are ill, or who must face specific challenges, or specific learning issues. These groups can often be incredibly helpful, offering information on all kinds of community resources for these families. As the world of home education expands, family resources are growing also, with new options and opportunities. So get involved; join one or more groups and discover some of these options. Then each family can choose what works for them, for their income resources, for their time resources, for their students' preferences. Because that is what home education is really all about -- fitting one's educational choices to each family's needs, each student's preferences. This is not a "one-size-fits-all" world and we don't nurture cookie cutter children.

Home education fits the education to the child, to the family, and that's what is so special about it. Sure, you will have to follow whatever state laws or regulations apply in your locale, but beyond that, the sky's the limit! Famous home schoolers have become MacArthur Fellowship winners, tennis champions, fencing champions, television and movie celebrities, published authors. You name it and whatever your children dream of doing, they can more readily achieve when brick and mortar walls no longer constrain their vision. Some home schoolers spend whole years on the road, traveling from place to place with their families. Some plan specific sojourns for weeks or months together, visiting other countries, doing interesting things, experiencing wonderful, often life-changing opportunities that they could never consider within the confines of institutional restrictions.

So join a group and if one doesn't exist, form a group. You can usually start with an online group, no matter where you live, as long as you have Internet access. What if you don't have Internet access? Most public libraries today provide computers and Internet access, many for free, so ask another homeschooler or your librarian to help you sign up for a free email address and start connecting. Link online with someone who can help you locate other home education groups in your area and keep searching until you find whatever works best for you. Don't restrict yourself to just one group, since you will learn from each group, whether you agree with every other member.

If you decide to form a group, even just a small neighborhood group to meet from time to time, base that decision on whatever seems appropriate for you and your family. Maybe you could handle a once a month meeting in a nearby park, or at the library, or your local "Y," or a church might offer space to you. You don't need to formally organize, either. These types of groups flow like water, changing as children mature and pursue their own interests, or as families move to new neighborhoods, get involved in different activities. So don't dismay if you notice changes in your group. Just "go with the flow" and adapt to changing circumstances. Your children's needs and interests will also continue changing, as your family's needs and interests evolve.

Life is full of surprises, so teaching your children how to adapt and adjust to change may be one of the best life lessons they will learn. Recognize that the same thing happens to children who attend brick and mortar schools. As new interests develop, children will make new friends, have less time for old friends, and life will turn in new and different directions. Of course, the difference is that brick and mortar students remain in the same classroom for nine months, with the same students, creating the illusion of stability. In this highly mobile society, with jobs that disappear faster than we can imagine, friends are going to move and students may need to make new friends all over again. This is perfectly okay and children need to know how to handle the kinds of changes that most can anticipate happening in their lifetimes.

# Bullying for Beginners

(Note: Discretion advised, this chapter might not be appropriate for young readers.)

*"Never be bullied into silence. Never allow yourself to be made a victim. Accept no one's definition of your life, but define yourself."-*
*Harvey S. Firestone*

The CDC reports that 15% of children who attend public and private high school have considered suicide. Worse yet, suicide among children ages 10-24 ranks as the third leading cause of death. Last year alone a number of children as young as 13 committed suicide in response to unrelenting bullying. Do students in the United States lack empathy, compassion, and consideration for anyone other than themselves? Does this lack of empathy, though not supported by public schools, somehow persist as a problem in schools due to the schools failing to educate students as whole individuals? Currently schools focus on producing students who can achieve high tests scores, even if that narrow-minded focus requires that they ignore clear warning signs of inappropriate and abusive behavior by students and sometimes faculty.

According to New Hampshire Family Life and Family Policy specialist, Malcolm Smith, who was a victim of bullying and who has been studying families and students for 30 years, this generation of students is meaner than generations before them. Malcolm Smith says that the current generation of kids is the meanest ever. Smith attributes the problem to parents who are not involved in their children's lives and to children not learning simple, basic values, like manners and kindness. I thought this very same thing long before any expert stepped forward and confirmed it. With almost daily news reports about violence in schools, shouldn't the public grasp that the current generation of school children are indeed the cruelest? I might have been bullied during my school days, but children today are tormented in school. The arrival of cell phones and social media websites only exacerbates the problem. Humiliation can now extend from school hallways to youtube.com, within the blink of an eye. Even as an adult, former friends and coworkers with a vendetta can post libelous statements about anyone on a public web page. And the law hasn't caught up with these types of crimes.

Bullying disseminates itself across social network websites like a wildfire, sweeping through people's lives, creating destruction and feelings of loss. These broadcasts erode and detrimentally impact the self esteem, relationships and friendships of those attacked. I can't imagine facing the possibility of such public torment while attending school each day. Bullies today will find any reason to lash out because they do lack manners, understanding and consideration, let alone kindness. And their families are not picking up the slack, either. When I was a teenager such things as camera phones and social websites did not exist. Had they existed I'm sure bullies would have taken full advantage of the technology to humiliate anyone they selected as a victim of their cruel intentions. Growing up I wasn't concerned about bullies having compromising photos of me or making untrue and cruel statements available for hundreds and thousands of people to read. I might not understand what motivates a bully's decision to torment another person, since I learned to always be kind and honest, but I do know that home educated students have very involved parents and usually learn strong values. With that in mind, I'm hoping that bullies don't pop up as often in the homeschool community. The hierarchical structure of public school, with its cliques that foster bullying, simply does not play such a big role in home education. In school cliques can label certain individuals as "popular," "the geek," or "the athlete," or worse. These social dichotomies can dominate the social scene in school, though not part of the curriculum. In the home education community learning usually takes precedence over social dichotomies. That said, however, one can always find someone, perhaps someone who recently left a public school setting, who overlays the bullying and clique mentality onto fellow home educators. But, as I mentioned above, parents are usually nearby and can respond promptly to the problem and deal with everyone involved. Schools still haven't figured out what to do, let alone how to deal with these problems.

One recent study published in Education Week finds a link between bullying and academic performance. Those students who suffered from bullying during the first year of high school saw a drop in their GPA by senior year. Most often minority students' grades decrease the most as the result of bullying. From the study it appears that in the long term minorities bear the greatest emotional and academic scars from bullying. This study clearly indicates that bullying in public institutions sustains an environment detrimental to learning. Public schools respond slowly to these types of situations and often fail to create proactive programs to prevent bullying. Only recently have some public schools started to support anti-bullying policies and programs. More often public schools consistently ignore or understate the problem. When public schooled students face issues of bullying, harassment and violence the victims often find few support staff who will help them, since many public schools can't afford trained counselors or mediators to deal with bullying.

I'm not excusing this lack of proper oversight in public schools, since the schools most often fail to follow through with appropriate programs involving moral values, guideposts, support, or consequences for individuals who threaten or harass peers. Many families who suffer the loss of a child due to suicide soon discover that their children were cruelly bullied while on school premises and faced school administrators who refused to take any responsibility for whatever happened.

On the other hand, home educated families often focus on their particular moral values, sometimes aligned with specific religious beliefs, and many pursue a rigorous academic curriculum that supports these moral values, often as part of the obligations and responsibilities required in the family environment. These family units integrate constructive activities into a functioning family unit with boundaries and clear consequences. While in a school environment children are often left to their own devices, without proper role models or clearly defined responsibilities for these types of actions. Surrounded by overburdened, stressed, and overworked faculty who lack the time or means to properly mediate these negative and destructive actions, young people find themselves relegated to peer groups, often cliques, stimulating an environment ripe for more bullying.

Without family support or community support many children resort to entertaining themselves, mainly through electronic communications, alcohol, or drug abuse, or sometimes by inflicting emotional or physical harm to themselves or others. Current research indicates that one out of every two publicly educated children will have suffered bullying, torment and sexual harassment by fellow students for reasons such as hair color, weight, height, family, poverty, religion, and sexuality. Many will succumb to sexual activity as early as the age of twelve or younger due to peer pressure. By the age of 18 the average publicly educated student will experience sexually explicit content, online bullying, pervasive language, while learning the least, and being held to the most mediocre of standards, all in a public education institution.

While attempting to get an education no student, no child, should feel so completely alone that suicide becomes a preferred choice. No child should face the threat of violence, sexual harassment, or torment over superficial characteristics, such as race, physical attributes, or sexual orientation. These qualities should be fostered as unique aspects of an intelligent individual. No child should be defined by and cruelly abused for something out of his or her control. Continuing to allow public institutions to educate children in such poor conditions condones bullying as an acceptable behavior.

Until public schools can effectively prevent bullying from happening, I see no reason to subject any child to these opportunities for potential emotional, physical, sexual and academic harm. Granted, a child will face adversity outside of the classroom, because hate exists everywhere. Prejudice, racism and cruelty persist in the world, like an uncontrollable pandemic. However, no child should face such injustices while in a facility that exists to educate him or her for a better life. What better life can originate from the harmful effects of rampant bullying? Since bullying often begins in lower grades and continues through high school, does this sound like the sort of education someone should receive in publicly funded institutions? Most people will face enough challenges through their lives as adults. Why would anyone want to allow the early childhood years to scar any child with these kinds of negative behaviors?

In 2007 in Mentor, Ohio, a 17 year old committed suicide after constant harassment at his high school. The teen suffered physical and verbal abuse while a student at Mentor High School. He was bombarded by gay slurs and shoved while on the school premises, most often while in math class. The student reported that the teacher of the class failed to protect him from the abuse. The young man ultimately shot himself due to the abuse he suffered in school. During that same year at Mentor High School, three other students committed suicide due to bullying, including a 16-year-old, who was relentlessly tormented and called "slutty." At her funeral the lovely young woman was laid to rest in her pink prom dress. When looking into the open casket the girls who had tormented her laughed. Is this the behavior you would want from your children? Is this why we are paying tax dollars to support public schools?

Then in 2010, in South Hadley, Massachusetts, a 15 year old girl committed suicide after constant torment from peers. The beautiful young woman spent months being bullied by "alpha" girls at her new school. Her mother contacted the school for help, but no one acted upon her complaint. On January 14, 2010, she hung herself with a scarf. Seven girls and two boys were charged in connection with her death. The girls were charged with criminal harassment and assault, and the boys for statutory rape. The school did not attempt to prevent the bullying that occurred while she was on school property. In the fall of 2010, after years of torment, a straight "A" student and eighth grader committed suicide by shooting himself in the head with his stepfather's pistol. Students at his school would act out gay sex acts in front of him, teased him for his religious beliefs, and the clothes he wore. No longer able to take it, this sweet, smiling boy took his own life. His parents were furious when the school later denied having any knowledge about their son being bullied. School officials blatantly lied about the parents ever contacting them, asking the school to help resolve the problem. Hopefully this story will remind parents to always leave a solid paper trail for any contact with the schools, including contacts regarding home education.

In 1999, two young men walked into their high school and killed 12 students and one teacher before committing suicide. Today the Columbine High School massacre remains as one of the worst school shootings. One year after that shooting Secret Service officials determined that bullying played a major role in 37 school shootings in the United States. You read that correctly: 37 school shootings. The majority of these shootings took place at high schools across the country. So, what conclusions could we draw from all this? Possibly that by high school age many bullied children have lost sight of any hope of a future free from torment, after years of harassment and shunning imposed on them in our schools. By high school age some of these bullied students have suffered this kind of torment for many years. Nothing ever excuses the behavior of any individual causing harm to another, unless in direct self defense, even if that individual had been bullied. However, as a culture we must accept responsibility for the role that bullying plays in violent events in our schools.

Yes, home educated students can turn into bullies and tormentors. However, the likelihood of a home educated student opening fire on a building full of children, children who by law must attend school, is much lower. Remember that these children are deemed truant if they don't attend school, thus they can't escape this type of violence, are captives to whatever violence they meet in their school settings. I've known a number of home schooled students who had ready access to firearms, due to a family propensity for hunting and 4-H. Yet, I haven't known a single one who either accidentally or intentionally shot another person. I strongly believe that the public school system creates an environment that cultivates feelings of despair, depression, and through shunning and ostracizing promotes loner tendencies. All of these are behaviors that could potentially precipitate acts of violence against others. Granted, not every depressed student will elect to kill other children at his or her school and many will persevere despite the bullying and go on to become successful adults. Honestly, the number of students who attend high schools compared to the relatively rare occurrences of shootings, fatalities, suicides, and incidents of violence might seem very low. But shouldn't even a single unnecessary death of a child be enough? How many of these types of deaths will we tolerate before we question our entire system of education?

I'm not a parent. I can't imagine losing a child, or the total terror of receiving a call or text from my child stating that there's a shooter in the school, nor the pain a parent must feel when a child suffers humiliation from peers on a regular basis. Though I can't

108

imagine it, I know that my own mother has spent sleepless nights worrying about me for much more mundane reasons. Having experienced bullying at a young age in school, I do know how it feels to get called names, shunned, and denied friendships. Among my publicly schooled friends such behavior was extremely common. During my teen years I saw firsthand how destructively and toxically teenagers can behave toward each other, spreading rumors about one another, even those involving sexually explicit interactions, as well as drug and alcohol abuse. Bullying experiences I witnessed preceded texting, "sexting," and camera phones, now so readily available to teens.

Those who bully will remain bullies because public school proves to them the effectiveness of bullying as a way to further oneself socially and academically. By adulthood some have learned how to badger others in many different venues, including the workplace and in online social networks where this type of bad behavior proliferates. Having not matured beyond the limited social interactions in public school, supported by peer pressure and dominated by bullying, the cycle continues. Most adults will never see themselves as bullies, nor will they notice this type of behavior in their children. So public schools will often remain factories, producing socially stunted young people with a compulsion for instant satisfaction, a dislike for learning, and at least a decade's worth of experiences that will have taught them how to bully or how to tolerate being bullied.

The stats don't lie when it comes to the emotional, physical and academic effects of bullying in the public schools today. According to the website MBNBD (Makebeatsnotbeatdowns.org), 87% of shootings were acts of revenge to "get back at those who have hurt them." Another statistic: 86% of students said they turn to lethal violence due to being made fun of and bullied. Approximately 160,000 children do not attend school every day out of fear of being attacked at school. Two-thirds, or 75%, of school shootings can be linked to bullying and harassment and 10% of students drop out of school due to bullying.

The sheer volume of statistics on the subject of bullying in schools continues to grow. Websites promoting anti-bullying slogans are also increasing. Sadly, so is the suicide rate of children 10-14 years old. Where do you draw the line and consider an alternative approach to education? Why force children to learn in a building in which some enter in fear every day? Why continue to convince families that the only way to get a proper and worthwhile education requires attendance at institutions that consistently fail to protect children? What will it take to question and consider something else, something better? Do you really want children to simply become statistics, numbers that indicate how terrifying their years in public school might be? What will it take? How long will you wait? Long enough for your child, for you, to become one of the 160,000 too afraid to go to school, or one out of 20 to see a gun at school. And, more likely, your child will be one of the 9 out of 10 victimized by bullying in school.

Consider an alternative and fight for a better education, instead of fighting to survive in a flawed and failing system. Recently a documentary took an intimate look at families directly impacted by bullying. In one family a child committed suicide as a direct result of relentless bullying. For another family their very young and sweet boy faced tormentors at school who beat him any way possible on the school bus ride, while the bus driver continued to drive and ignored the abuse. Within the walls of many schools such abuse often thrives, unnoticed in bathroom stalls, hallways, or school parking lots. Students face each day in constant fear of getting hit, taunted, and tormented. When did attending school mean facing the potential for physical and emotional harm?

We continue to raise our children to believe in the importance of learning and train them to think that schools are the best place to learn. Families are brainwashed into believing that education and learning can only succeed in a classroom at a school. Schools fail to tell us many of the other less than pleasant things that routinely occur within those very same classroom walls. How much learning really takes place? How much bullying does each child really face? Will a school ever honestly answer those questions? Will a school ever truly deal with the concerns of parents? So far it appears that school systems are good at one thing: evading the truth. Yet those very same people involved in deceiving families about the safety and effectiveness of schools are the ones strongly advocating against home education. Maybe those people want children to suffer? At the very least, we know that schools want the tax dollars usually allocated for each student in a district. Criticism of home education doesn't originate solely because educators and administrators perceive it as an inferior form of education, but rather because it takes money away from school districts and districts are scrambling for every dollar they can scrounge these days.

The effects of bullying can extend past just simple teasing and taunting in grade school or high school. Bullying remains an issue well into adulthood. Workplace bullying causes substantial financial losses for companies. In the workplace some studies estimate that employers lose $19 billion annually because of bullying, and another $3 billion due to the impact bullying and fear of bullying bears on productivity. Those who bully are six times more likely to find themselves incarcerated by the age of 24. Long term emotional and physical effects from bullying will cut short or derail the amazing lives of many young people. Long term costs for those incarcerated young people already reaches into the tens of billions. When will we stand up to bullying and the schools for allowing bullying to continue? When will families recognize that children shouldn't suffer from bullying? With other legal options available, no one should acquiesce, allowing a school to bully parents or students into thinking they will best educate every child.

Schools possess neither the time nor resources to take on the issues of bullying. Parent involvement is critical in preventing bullying, but schools set themselves up to separate the parent from the child by design. This creates a dissonance in the family structure that frequently degrades communication. And poor communication can prevent a child from speaking up when hurt and when needing to get a parent or an adult's attention to curtail bullying. If parents were present for each moment of the eight hours most children spend in school, fully present and aware of the child's actions, a bullying child would face more consistent consequences and recognition of behavioral issues long before that child could ever destroy the lives of other children. Home education removes the walls between parent and child, opening communication and consequences for the immediate situation, at the very moment an incident takes place. In a way home education could solve the problem of bullying entirely. But, we won't know for sure until we try; and considering the alternative, I'd say it would be well worth the effort.

Potentially both girls and boys will bully each other. In the case of girls bullying other girls they tend to initiate psychological pain through manipulation, peer pressure and personal criticism. Female bullies might not always stoop to physically harming their victims, but the emotional pain inflicted within tightly knit groups or cliques of girls that can last a life time. Tendencies of young women to cruelly spread rumors about other women for selfish and petty reasons might not bruise the flesh, but often hurts one's emotional being. Institutionally educated girls who must face the competitive and shallow nature of their peers, especially those who mainly focus on attracting male sexual partners instead of learning, can inflict considerable emotional damage on their victims. Such behavior frequently ends with girls teasing and taunting one another, and sometimes initiating physical altercations over competition for dating partners. Bullying for boys usually involves physical violence, like shoving, kicking, pulling hair and punching each other.

Along with the same kinds of physical abuse, male bullies taunt with cruel statements to their victims, frequently regarding their sexuality, or lack of masculinity. Both genders sharpen their psychological and physical abuse skills very well during their years within school walls.

One could further attribute an increase in bullying and "bullycide" (the term used for suicides caused by relentless bullying) to increased technology. Using cell phone cameras and social networking websites, an embarrassing moment suddenly escalates from something a small group of friends might view to a photograph posted publicly to hundreds or thousands, even millions of strangers. If you no longer like someone you can post a photo of them and post cruel comments about that person for hundreds of online "friends" to read. Consequences for such actions seldom directly impact the bully. He or she doesn't face each victim. These technological tools have raised the stakes of bullying to a higher degree of viciousness, one that is faceless, voiceless, and yet can wreak serious emotional damage.

Even after death victims' families still struggle with the effects of bullying when comments made online about their child remain viewable. We live in a world where bullying can dominate everyday conversation. In schools witnesses to bullying rarely intervene, for fear of reprisal and because they have so frequently witnessed so much bullying that they hesitate to do anything but avoid these situations. Often other students simply stand by and watch while bullies attack victims. In school too many students accept that bullying serves a purpose, believe that they can't avoid this malicious aspect of the school experience. The majority of students simply accept bullying because, well, children will be children. I'm not sure about you, but if I knew my child had bullied another child I would not just shrug it off. I would also not place my child in an environment where he or she would face potential abuse from peers. The very nature of schools inherently fosters exactly the type of hierarchical pecking order that perfectly sustains bullying.

With little adult supervision and rampant stereotyping, peer groups divided by age, gender, race, and socioeconomic status can spark negative social situations and interactions. Since school students sort themselves according to these superficial social constructs some children will always elevate themselves, assuming positions of superiority. Segregating by specific characteristics like this only raises the likelihood of peer judgment and taunting. In the school environment where these cliques form some children will always "fit in" while others will find themselves outcasts. While attempting to fit in children may sacrifice parts of their individual identities. They may struggle to form meaningful connections with others. But instead, these bullying groups degrade the emotional stability, intelligence and well being of vulnerable students. Each day in school a child will face whether to be a bully, a bystander, or a victim. Attending an institution to learn should not require such decisions. Children should be choosing what they'd like to learn, not fearing how school attendance will harm them.

# The "S" Word (Socialization)

*"I am convinced there is only one way to eliminate these grave evils, namely through the establishment of a socialist economy, accompanied by an educational system which would be oriented toward social goals. In such an economy, the means of production are owned by society itself and are utilized in a planned fashion. A planned economy, which adjusts production to the needs of the community, would distribute the work to be done among all those able to work and would guarantee a livelihood to every man, woman, and child. The education of the individual, in addition to promoting his own innate abilities, would attempt to develop in him a sense of responsibility for his fellow men in place of the glorification of power and success in our present society" - Albert Einstein*

Rumors abound about how home educated children never develop normal social skills. Whoever started such rumors probably never spoke to an actual home educated student and just assumed that only in a traditional public school setting could children effectively interact socially. In my experience home educated students relate well to a much wider age range than those in traditional school environments. I can't remember a moment in my life when I couldn't readily converse with new people and initiate new friendships. Usually I would discover that I was at least better educated, more cultured, and often more mature than my peers. However, I still faced the same issues, the same dating problems, the same peer pressures and the same angst.

During my early years as an unschooler I spent a great deal of time in a wide variety of social situations. My mom allowed me to organize events and "clubs" around my interests, so I was meeting up with my peers on a regular basis. At this same busy time I was focusing on my passion for competitive figure skating, usually practicing 2-4 hours a day at the ice rink. Unschooling meant that I could train for figure skating while other skaters attended school, so when I skated during the day I seldom hung out with skaters my own age. If I was resting during Zamboni breaks, I passed my off-ice time talking to the rink staff, ice skating instructors, and other adult ice skaters who also practiced during the day and who expected me to behave like an adult, not a child.

I never felt different or socially disadvantaged. Sometimes the subject of school would arise when someone in my social circle would mention what he or she disliked about school and I would quip about how I didn't deal with that sort thing. Of course, that remark would garner a flurry of questions, to which I would explain that I was home educated. One of the most frequent responses I heard, especially from other adults, was, "I never would have thought that you were home schooled."

According to the stereotype home educated kids behave as if their super religious parents lock them away in a basement. On the outside home educated students don't usually appear any different from other students. However, we constantly fight the stigma of very cruel rumors about our supposed lack of social skills. Nearly all the home educated friends I've known over their growing-up years have gracefully assimilated into the popular cultures of college and adulthood. Although I should note that many return to public school for their critical last two to four high school years. During those over-hyped teenage years many home educated students cave to peer pressure, compelling them to participate in the traditional teen coming of age rituals by returning to the brick and mortar classroom, instead of sticking with home education.

For that matter, those high school years probably provoke the highest percentage of home education "dropouts." Many home educated students elect to involve themselves in team sports, proms and graduation. Granted, there aren't many organized sports teams for home educated students, but home schoolers participate in some awesome Frisbee golf teams, chess competitions, and spelling bees. Some master amazing individual sports, too, like fencing, Tae Kwan Do, gymnastics, tennis (like Vanessa and Serena Williams), skiing, and my favorite, figure skating. But for some teens, the appeal of spending their high school years among peers in a group setting strongly draws them back to school.

Often my friends would inquire about why I didn't want to go to school and if I didn't feel like I was missing out? I never understood this question since I couldn't figure out exactly what they thought I might have missed. Through volunteering I met my first "boyfriend," the guy I dated during my peak high school years while I continued to train on the ice for competitive figure skating. My social life reached an apex at 16 while I was attending a Unitarian church with my family. At that time their large youth group generated many close friendships. The only thing I missed was sitting in classes and taking all those mandated state tests. Without a doubt, I participated in all the other typical teen activities, like working at a part time job, fulfilling an active social life on weekends, attending parties, dating, boyfriends, attending school dances (as a guest at an assortment of public, private and parochial schools in our metropolitan area), sports, friendships, late night outings to get ice cream, and sleepovers. No one ever wondered about my education or thought I was a weird kid. In retrospect, most people considered me a "popular" teen, at least when compared to some typical institutionalized learning standards.

If you had met me back then when I was with my friends, you would never have noticed any difference. I looked like any other teen spending time at the mall, at the movie theater, at the park, etc. I never overheard anyone making snide remarks about my lack of personality or social skills. My friends enjoyed my company and, as usual, everyone I met would act surprised to hear that I was indeed home educated. I considered that a compliment. I recognize that people will always criticize home education and always believe that home educated students will not develop properly, or "normally." If I could, I would ask those people just how properly developed and socialized they find all those students who attend public school, especially those who bully their peers mercilessly? Maybe my definition of developing into an adult doesn't coincide with the ideals of others. Personally I prefer that those who demonstrate genuine social skills demonstrate care and consideration, that they treat others nicely.

While not lacking friends during my home educated preteen and teenage years, in my early schooling years, especially while I was attending public schools, things differed considerably. I was born and raised in rural New Mexico, in a tiny community in the high desert mountains. In my last year attending public school I felt completely ostracized and alienated from my peers. Just two years earlier my family had intended to move to the Midwest, but plans fell through. Instead of re-enrolling in the school I had attended my mom transferred me to a public elementary school down the road, where a close family friend taught. This required special permission from the school district, based on my mother's complaint about a rather nasty "incident" I had faced at my assigned school. That year I injured my left humerus, broke it clean though, in a serious playground bullying incident. A girl at that school had harassed me by grabbing my legs and swinging them around as I hung from some horizontal ladder bars on the playground, keeping up her bullying until I finally fell to the ground and suffered a broken arm. My mom, furious with the school for its failure to appropriately handle this matter, as well as its failure to adequately staff the playground, requested a transfer to the only other elementary school on our side of the mountains. This placed me at an immediate disadvantage. I hung out in the classroom with my teacher during recess time because the school refused to even let me go out and sit outside with friends, for liability reasons.

So I spent those first few months getting to know my teacher. I mostly read, completed homework, and chatted about what we were studying. By the time my arm had healed enough that I could join the other students on the playground during recess, I had learned to rather like my teacher. But several other students in my class decided that our teacher preferred me over some of them, accusing me of being "the teacher's pet." I would never have chosen to spend my recess sitting in the classroom, but somehow my situation led my peers to believe that I was a "kiss-up" and that our teacher favored me. Through no fault of my own, since I most definitely did not choose to break my arm, I remained in the classroom, frustrated, thinking that this social ostracism was stupid. By the time I could return to the playground, could join the other students without a cast on my arm, they had cast me as a social pariah, not worthy of friendship because I had received "special" privileges while healing from my injury. Though I never received compassion or understanding from my classmates, I still attempted to make friends. My mom even planned parties for me, encouraging me to invite students from my school, and she also volunteered to drive us on field trips, hoping her presence would somehow give me the support to eek out just a little friendly footing from my classmates. Since I was shy to begin with, my injury had set me outside the normal school-based social circles. I tried Girl Scouts to make friends, but met with the same ostracism. Then I tried 4-H and surprisingly discovered that my local 4-H club, over 100 families strong, consisting primarily of homeschoolers, were a very friendly bunch.

By the end of the fourth grade most of my classmates shunned me, so I felt unpopular, alone and friendless. I had somehow committed the worst of offenses, by being different, the girl with a cast on her arm. Even though what made me different was entirely temporary and superficial, my social ostracism, due to

119

circumstances beyond my control, often left me despondent, disinterested, and completely frustrated. During the following summer I spent time with the children of family friends, some older and some younger, none of whom I had met at school. I also participated in 4-H activities and competitions. I did very well in 4-H, bringing home stacks of blue ribbons and purple rosettes, even a few trophies. But since most of my 4-H friends did not attend school, I was still an outsider at school.

Before finally moving to the Midwest I attended a couple of weeks of fifth grade at that same school. The pattern established in fourth grade remained. Through rumors and peer pressure those same girls simply refused to acknowledge my existence. I spent my last few recesses playing alone on the farthest playground. Sometimes I cried when I came home, wondering what terrible sin I had committed to be so totally rejected? I was a really shy kid, personable, but still shy. I was the kid who clung to her mom's pants while out shopping when I was very young. For me being shy meant that I tried that much harder to befriend other kids. Yet, I still found myself friendless and cruelly shunned.

I'm sure my story sounds familiar. For that matter, compared to what some children in schools today have faced, my experience was not so bad. When I decided to tell my story about my unschooling experience I hoped that readers would grasp that socializing in public schools isn't necessarily something to brag about and can very adversely stunt one's interactions and one's development of social skills. Clearly, those girls at my public elementary school were bullies, and, as such, failed to exhibit good social skills. Maybe it's just me, because I believe that social skills require someone to demonstrate that they can relate and understand another human being. Maybe bullying, shunning others, and destroying the self esteem of peers, for no reason at all, have replaced consideration and concern for others as skills every child should learn.

Recently, as an adult, I've realized something interesting. During my teenage years I struggled, often feeling shy in social situations. I chalked this up to my years of home education. What I didn't realize then, that I definitely realize now, is that many people suffer from feeling uncomfortable or shy in social situations, especially during their teen years. Unfortunately many hide this by getting high or drinking, or both, before they go out, or while they are out.

Home education helped my parents understand what was happening in my life, day-to-day, and yes, sometimes that felt smothering. However, I strongly believe that their involvement and constant presence in my life, as my main support and as authority figures and role models, kept me from getting involved with alcohol and drugs when so many of my friends and acquaintances readily succumbed to these temptations. My parents weren't unnecessarily strict, but they instilled in me a sense of accountability and responsibility for my own actions, so I learned how to be socially active without the usual teen excursions into substance abuse of one kind or another.

Now, as a young adult, I consider myself fairly well adjusted. Though I may not look any different than my publicly schooled peers, I can vouch for the differences inside. No one has ever approached me and said, "Hey, you must have been home schooled; I can tell, you just aren't well socialized." When people meet students who sport labels like "weird," "freak," "crazy," or who might be threatening harm, no one's first thought about these kids is, "Oh, hey, I bet that kid was home educated." Honestly, you very rarely hear about a home educated student bully, or a home educated student lighting another student's hair on fire, or hanging them up on fences, or berating and humiliating someone until, in utter despair, that student victim might resort to suicide. In case you didn't know, all of those things have shown up in headlines lately and one can locate plenty of news stories supporting how bullying behavior has pushed some students to the unthinkable point of self-destruction. Most of these suicides in the past few years, usually provoked by events that took place in public schools, or precipitated by students in those schools, slip through the cracks, unnoticed until too late.

Now I'll admit, maybe not enough of us truly grasp whether we exhibit strong antisocial tendencies. I mean, with millions of children in traditional schools, only a small percentage resort to bullying, with fewer still who end up as mass murderers. Did you hear about the student who lit another child's hair on fire? Or about the one who threw unopened coke cans at a child's head? What about the student locked in a closet for so long she urinated all over herself after removing her clothing in desperation to keep her clothes from getting wet? All of those events occurred in public schools or on school buses while under the supervision of school personnel. In most cases school employees stand idly nearby while students torment and humiliate other students, perpetrating these punitive acts against vulnerable students. At a Texas high school officials met to discuss changing a policy that restricts male employees from spanking female students to administer punishment. If the policy changes young girls at the high school will face paddling on their bottoms behind closed-doors with only men present. Surely this approach to misbehavior stirs up more problems than it solves.

Since home educated students enjoy parental supervision, usually around the clock, behaving well comes naturally. Arguments will still arise, but not when both parents and children are exhausted from eight hours away from home, and not during the only time a family spends together after all those hours at work and school. Personally I appreciated my constant parental supervision as I went through my teenage years.

When parents support students and set clear boundaries, instead of punishing students with rules designed to maintain the appearance of order and control, students can mature into adults with strong social skills. Parents sacrifice the eight hours a child usually spends away from home and in school, time when they could be working, or pursuing an advanced college degree, or starting a business. Instead these dedicated parents opt to spend that time with their child or children. Let me tell you, home-educating parents sacrifice a great deal and hope to raise intelligent, creative, bright, shining, friendly children. No one gives up all that free time and "free babysitting," as my mom calls it, to raise a child who grows into a complete failure and screw-up. Assuming home educated children don't know how to interact well with others insults the families who dedicate all that time and money to support and organize social opportunities for their home schooled children.

Truthfully, some families who home educate do so because they want their children to learn about certain alternative ideas about science, such as those that question evolution. These ideas could isolate their children and can prevent exposure to alternate ways of thinking. However, those children almost always participate in their own church and other community activities. Personally I oppose forcing any one theory or doctrine on a child. Parents must choose the moral code, rules, guidelines, or doctrines suited best to their family. What often encourages a child to play and positively engage with others develops from parental involvement. My maturity and intelligence developed from my parents and the time we spent together, not from just sending me to school, expecting teachers to handle everything. I attribute being a caring and kind person to my parents and to my years of unschooling during which I learned to think for myself.

Home education will not stunt or damage a child when parents incorporate social opportunities and a more inclusive and open-minded attitude toward everyday life. On its own, home education doesn't foster antisocial tendencies. Through constant and daily communication with parents, siblings, and each other, home educated children probably socialize more than the average publicly educated child. Home educating organizations, with hundreds to thousands of member families, regularly schedule a wide selection of social events. From field trips, parties, book exchanges, science fairs, spelling bees, ski clubs, roller skating, and so much more, students can choose what they like, participate as much or as little as they deem appropriate. As I mentioned, no one noticed anything different about me. I look like any other normal college graduate who holds a job, and regularly goes out with friends. My friends don't notice anything different or lacking in my social skills. Not a single person wonders about the education I experienced before college. I get along well with everyone I meet and enjoy a life surrounded by interesting, talented and creative friends.

No single approach to education will fit every family and not every home educated student will mature into an individual who positively contributes to his or her community, but the same applies to publicly educated children. Home educating creates great communicators who can usually discuss a multitude of topics and interests. Through discussions on science, art, chess, music, etc., I acquired the social skills I needed to get a job and maintain it, to attend college and succeed in my studies there. Home educating presented me with a diverse group of people from whom I was always learning. For example, when I was volunteering at our local natural history museum or teaching school children how to make candles at our local historical village, I engaged in interactive situations with a wide range of people, of all ages and backgrounds. During the years when I worked multiple jobs and volunteered I conversed with coworkers and visitors from all over the world. When students limit discussions and talk only with those the same age, or from similar socioeconomic backgrounds, this limits conversations to whatever interests that one group. In school I certainly witnessed how no one would dare to talk to the different child, the one with interesting and creative ideas to share. At an early age I realized the value of listening to others, especially those who differed greatly from me. Now I happily enjoy friendships that include younger and older individuals, people from all over the world, and those who don't share my same perspective, but who still deserve my respect and interest. In many careers interpersonal skills and the ability to relate well to a diverse group of people determines success and the potential for promotions. Frequently I notice young people focus on themselves and the limited interests of their peers and don't bother acknowledging or talking to someone older or from a different background. I pity those young people who miss out on the knowledge they could be sharing with others who could contribute to their broader understanding of their community and the world.

Every so often the life drawing studio I attend will offer a free night when high school students can join the group and draw. I looked forward to this shared experience, excited about this opportunity for young artists to observe and participate, to draw with experienced local artists. The usual group of extremely talented artists at these studio sessions range in age from their early twenties well into their sixties and seventies. Many support themselves with their art as established professional artists, award winners, gallery owners and university professors. I expected these high school students would question the other studio artists about college, technique, materials, etc. Instead the students kept to themselves, missing out on a great opportunity to gain some amazing knowledge about art. From my perspective this demonstrated a lack of social skills from these "properly schooled" students who ignored everyone else in the room and chatted only amongst themselves. Unable to socially acclimate to this new and challenging environment, these students failed to benefit from the wealth of information available in that studio.

Those who aren't venturing beyond their own small social sphere overlook many potential opportunities to connect to others. Public schools do not teach children social skills. Critics can say whatever they would like about the unsocialized home educated student, but they fail to mention that schools don't intend to be social institutions. For that matter, most schools avoid that distinction, or rebuke it completely. Schools subsist to educate the student and most teachers maintain that while in class students do not talk to each other. Teachers dictate silence and obedience, even stillness (no wiggling). I've seen how publicly educated students can't socially engage with anyone who isn't from their same social milieu, relating only to those who are socially, economically, and in many other ways just like themselves. They never look beyond the limited sphere of their own peer interests, thus missing out on the wealth of knowledge, beauty and wonder that prevail all around them. If you think about it, that makes them the disadvantaged and socially stunted ones, who have failed to acquire adequate social skills.

During my preteen and teen years my social life revolved around friends who attended public schools and a few who enrolled in private schools. I found that many of these peers demanded a great deal of attention from both friends and family and thrived on creating plenty of drama. More rebellious than I, my publicly educated acquaintances often engaged in sexual promiscuity, alcohol and drug use, reckless driving, bullying, gossiping, and other self destructive behavior. Most of the young girls focused on finding a boyfriend, while the young men immersed themselves in violent video games on various gaming systems. Their families often appeared splintered and distant from my perspective. At times certain parents passed the buck, expecting the schools to teach their children personal responsibility, abdicating their parental responsibilities and failing to establish clear behavior boundaries.

Granted, not all publicly educated families resemble those I met. By contrast the home educated children I knew were very family focused, highly intelligent and involved in a multitude of academic and/or athletic activities, leaving little time for the usual teen rebellion. Many parents would often wonder how my mom could tolerate spending so much time around me, all day, every day, or how I stood my mom as my primary "teacher." Didn't we make each other miserable, they'd ask? Wouldn't so much time around my mom turn me into a socially stunted adult with attachment issues? Though many people judged and criticized my unschooling education and tried to convince my mother that I would grow up with the social skills of a wet rag, the truth is that I grew up and assimilated quite well into the "real world."

I've never struggled to find a job, nor have I ever been fired from a job. I've maintained strong friendships and relationships throughout my life, so far. One week after graduating from college I started working for a test scoring center. After only one year, my social skills, work ethic, and job performance earned me a promotion to a supervisory position as a Team Leader. At the age of 24 my responsibilities expanded to overseeing and training a team of up to ten people. No one criticized me or told me that I'm not social enough, or that I needed to improve my social skills. None of my managers or supervisors reprimanded me for any behavioral issues. How many people can say that? I think that only proves that despite what most would consider a very unorthodox education, I wasn't affected negatively by it at all. I still work and succeed at my job. I'm able to supervise and manage a team of mostly older adults, or to teach a group of children from ages 4-16 how to ice skate. The social skills that I learned during my home education years shaped me into the capable and friendly person I am today.

I've proven that an unschooled student can learn to live a successful and active social life, like every other student, simply through living life well. If your greatest fear about home education stems from fears that it will isolate and will detrimentally limit the social skills of a child, I hope my personal experiences will put those fears to rest. I've always made friends and enjoy a very active social calendar. Trust me; I'm not the only home educated adult who has reaped the rewards of not attending school. Every home educated adult I know enjoys the same activities, friendships, and relationships as his or her publicly schooled peers. I haven't heard of one who lived a life of complete social isolation, or who lived at home in the basement. I honestly know more publicly educated students who struggle to find close friends, who grow up into emotionally struggling adults, or who simply don't relate well with others.

Some of my publicly schooled friends have grown into shallow, self-satisfying adults, who only focus on intimate relationships or financial success and rarely take any interest or pleasure in building affirming and honest friendships with others. If nothing can be gained from a "friendship" and if it isn't someone he or she can use for various reasons, then he or she will not waste any time fostering more than a purely superficial connection. If that sounds like the type of adult you'd like to raise, then unschooling won't work for you. Unschooling opens the opportunities for individual growth beyond the superficial, cruel and often narcissistic qualities that dominate many public school environments. The unschooler's social experiences can explore connections beyond the simple peer-to-peer relationships found in a school. While unschooling a child can learn how to engage with those from all age groups, cultures and socioeconomic backgrounds, while making deeper and richer friendships based on mutual interests, respect, and understanding, instead of appearances, ethnicities or materialistic values.

In my mind the entire idea of socialization encompasses following a set of strong values and morals that mold someone into a person who contributes to his or her community and family. Socialization should focus on positive characteristics, like kindness, honesty, a love for learning, and a desire to help others, while also fostering genuine connections and learning. If you consider public school as the only place where a child can properly learn social skills then you should be terrified about the sort of adults some schools are turning loose in our world. In recent years those "well socialized" children getting educated in public schools have bullied many children to death, literally, through suicide and even homicide.

Perhaps people need to re-evaluate what socialization means. The unschooling child can learn the importance of communicating well with others and by doing so can establish strong social skills. Many young people today lack effective communication skills, because opportunities in which good communication takes precedence rarely exist in public schools. Instead many students substitute social media sites, texting, and instant messaging which weaken the ability to communicate. These students often accept those who talk only in little broken down bits that carry little to no meaning and resemble nothing more than nonsensical strings of letters. Developing social skills only occurs when one person actively interacts with another person. In real conversations a person experiences a push and pull, an exchange of thoughts, while ideas and stories unfold, leading to expanded vocabulary, to learning about opposing or interesting and different points of view. All of this folds into the creation of a socially well adjusted individual.

In my personal life meeting people from all over the country and all over the world, from Israel to Haiti, from Utah to Michigan, and from every possible religious, political and racial background, I discovered the importance of humility, honesty, and hope. Finding common ground between me and others has broadened my social skills. Publicly educated students very often isolate themselves with their ipods, laptops, and social cliques. Loneliness subsists like an invisible disease behind those silent faces, with the music turned up, the fake smiles in the hallway, and the "friends" with whom we click to connect on social networking sites. Whatever social skills you might think automatically attach to children in public school often develop into nothing more than how to connect on the most basic of levels. Children learn how to accept loneliness and disappear, so they won't get bullied on the school bus ride home. Some learn how to maintain an acceptable facade with make-up or clothes, while disregarding individual expression in the hopes of gaining hollow attention or shallow affection from others.

Aim for something better, for a social landscape that encourages goals and expression, creativity, thoughtfulness, excitement, and resilience. Cultivate one that expands one's potential circle of friendships, of places to go, and of beautiful things to discover beyond the vapid skin deep interactions available between the walls of many schools. Unschooling can cultivate amazing social activities and lifelong growth. So, don't worry that home education or unschooling will stunt a child's social growth. I was unschooled and I definitely don't have any long term psychological damage from not attending a public school spending my days around other children the same age, from the same general neighborhood. I know that this won't convince many people. I know that many can't imagine that a child can grow into a normal, healthy and intelligent adult with normal, intelligent friends. I prove that one can maintain good personal relationships and an active social life, and turn into a person who doesn't obviously differ from any other person, especially from those who did attend a public school.

If anyone learns anything from this chapter, I hope that just because something is different doesn't mean it's not as good. Just because unschooling approaches educating a child differently doesn't mean that it will harm anyone. Every choice a person makes includes a calculated amount of risk. But without taking a risk no one would ever learn to drive, to love, to swim, or to dance. So, take a risk that maybe, just possibly, unschooling might foster a socially happy child, a child who can strike up a conversation with anyone, who loves to share with family and friends. I believe that I grew up into the kind of person who doesn't define my self worth by how popular I am, but by the close bonds I have made with others. Now, that's the kind of socialization every child needs.

# The Monetary School

*"By preventing a free market in education, a handful of social engineers - backed by the industries that profit from compulsory schooling: teacher colleges, textbook publishers, materials suppliers, et al. - has ensured that most of our children will not have an education, even though they may be thoroughly schooled."*
*– John Taylor Gatto*

      Designed to fulfill required curricular standards, the public education system educates children through a set curriculum, approved by an educational board.  This curriculum rarely changes because the public education system debates and argues about possible changes for years before applying any innovation or implementing technology in the classroom.  Even with generous gifts, like the ones Bill and Melinda Gates have donated to many districts, schools still hesitate to introduce innovation.  Thus the vast technological resources of the Internet, an easy portal to new educational approaches via the web, with engaging lesson plans, as well as instant access to newer texts and other interactive learning options, might never arrive in the institutional classroom.

      Unschooling and home education effectively and efficiently open resources for families to access a wide variety of learning options without spending much money.  Unlike the traditional school setting, where students and teachers lose a great deal of time shuffling from one class to another, quieting down the rowdy students (who should probably try unschooling), those who educate at home effectively jump right into actual learning activities, at any time of day, whenever it works best for them and their families.  Even though many school districts beg the public for increased school levies and taxes every year as the administrators plead that they lack funding and can't afford basic school necessities, staff, fuel for buses, or new technological advances, students still don't experience the best education possible. If public schools effectively "educated," then surely a far greater percentage of students attending would graduate and go on to college. Also, it would not take twelve years of forced education to produce students who often end up poorly prepared for even the most basic jobs.

Federal funding for schools, based on the students' test scores that supposedly rate school performance, can quickly punish underperforming schools by shrinking federal funding when they fail to meet the academic standards state and federal agencies establish. So if a school performs badly, then it receives less money. That seems like a perfectly reasonable approach, right? What about the following scenario: a little boy loves math, but with too few math books in his classroom his teacher can't assist him, so the little boy struggles with his assignments and fails his math tests. As the little boy grows up in the public school system he continues to struggle and faces the emotional burden of never doing well. Therefore the system punishes the child. If the student scores poorly on a test the school loses money and less money usually means even fewer supplies, fewer teachers, and a higher student to teacher ratio in classrooms.

Students must score well on certain tests, the ones that the state believes will prove or disprove the performance level of a school. Since every state sets different standards a child who might fail in one state could pass or be a "C" or better student in another state. Every state decides its own guidelines, and yet every state receives funding at the federal level based upon their completely different state proficiency tests. For example, the standards set for passing a graduation test in the state of Wisconsin might differ considerably from those in nearby Illinois. Unschooling doesn't necessarily solve every issue, but it surely does open the possibility of a better alternative, a fairer educational experience for more children. Every child deserves to learn in a way that enriches and supports his or her individual educational needs.

I began teaching ice skating to children when I was 17. Figure skaters compete aggressively, and so do the instructors who charge an average hourly wage of anywhere between $20-$200. Often instructors completely ignore the child's well being and safety, fail to include injury prevention training, nor offer health/anatomy studies as part of the skater's training. When profit motives preside, then the importance of proper training often slips down the list. Not only can one find many unqualified instructors, those who lack any real previous skating or competition experience, but those who offer little to no knowledge of anatomy or physiology, both of which are important for any sports related field of work. Since each skating instructor approaches teaching differently, based on his or her own perspective and personal experience, whatever approach he or she chooses cannot possibly work with every skater. Figure skating instructors can manipulate and persuade parents, telling them what they want to hear, that their child will, of course, do very well and will only succeed with their instruction.

Public education advocates long ago mastered the art of persuasion in this way, and for the same reason. Money drives our society, and often, like my example about ice skating instruction, money determines the quality or lack of quality that you receive. School systems put levies on their local ballots appealing for more money every year. They hold fundraisers, request donations from alumni, seek out corporate sponsors, and persuade prospective families that their school district is the best. What are they not saying, though? First they aren't revealing that for every student that enrolls at their institution they receive federal, local and state money. Did you just ask yourself, "They get more money?" This might blow your mind a little bit, but in one state the amount of money spent to educate a single student for one year averages just over $17,000.

Yes, you read correctly: $17,000 for one student for one year in elementary through secondary school, more than twice what it costs college undergrads to attend many universities for a year of in-state tuition at a public college or university. I'm sure public schools aren't teaching college level courses to 4th and 5th graders. Does every U.S. school get that much money per student? No. New York receives the most per student, a total of over $53 million in funds for the entire state, or $17,173 per student. States such as Utah, Idaho and Arizona sit on the lower end of the scale, coming in at $5765-$7608 per student. Do student test scores and the quality of education reflect these funding differences? Of course they do. Personally I believe even $5000 per student per year is excessive. Did I mention the part about how a school receives state, local, and federal funding per student enrolled? That's right; I did. Schools spend money for teachers, supplies, facilities, buses, fuel, food, staff, etc. If a family chooses to home educate their child then the school does not receive money for that child.

So, if you're a public school board member and you're trying to balance your budget, you're going to try to find ways to get more money. Many will argue that public school's opposition to unschooling and homeschooling stems from unqualified parent teachers, lack of socialization, poor performance and inability to acclimate well, find a job, or attend college. If you really researched these points I think you would find that if a school can get another $17,000, or even just another $5,000 added to their bloated budgets, simply by enrolling one more student, then they will, of course, demonize anything that interferes with their ability to receive that money. I mean, come on, honestly, if they really cared about the well-being of children they would advocate much more strongly for parent involvement, healthy food in schools, and safer buildings. Also public institutions would enforce stronger anti-bullying policies. They would care about and create stronger connections to the community through volunteering. Public schools would educate students, preparing them for college, helping them learn job skills while encouraging them to excel and maybe even graduate early. If they really cared about the students they would do everything in their power to provide the best education possible.

U.S. public school systems currently hold over $377 million in outstanding debt, despite receiving annual funding from both the state and federal government. Local school districts must resort to school levies in a desperate attempt to stay in the black. Many small rural districts can't afford school bus service, sometimes cut driver's education programs, music programs, AP courses, eliminate school counselors who help students with college and job training information, hitting these school districts the hardest. Some schools can't afford a certified school librarian and this prevents children from even using the school library. Yes, you read that correctly. Though a school building may contain a library, the students may not get to use it due to the bureaucratic and contractual restraints of the public school system. All of this adds up to a perpetual cycle of failing schools and, worst yet, students ill-equipped for the future. Often you hear on news reports about teachers buying school supplies for their classrooms, using their own money because many school children in impoverished areas can't afford the required basic school supplies. In some schools the classroom books are outdated, destroyed, falling apart or missing completely, so students share a few copies. Schools lacking a library, or the funding to transport students to a library, limit student access to information in a system supposedly designed to educate them.

Public schools restrict students to studying only certain subjects and following a very specific path based almost entirely on age or on the results of often poorly written exams. Many students fail exams because the teacher never had time to cover everything needed to properly prepare them, or the student can't read and comprehend the questions. In the workplace if employees consistently perform poorly they face job loss or must complete training modules to improve their performance. Schools do neither; they don't fire (aka expel students) for poor grades, and rarely do they offer opportunities for self improvement, leaving some students between a rock and a hard place. Unable to technically find another learning situation better suited to that student, because of state truancy laws, a student must often remain in a frustrating, or even a failing situation. Essentially schools force students to struggle. Public schools care more about enrollment numbers than intellectual needs. I'm not saying that schools should start expelling students doing poorly. I'm saying that schools don't give those students any other option besides keeping them in the school, despite obvious learning issues.

Home educated children never receive any of the public and federal money allocated to students who enroll in public schools. Still, home schooling and unschooling families pay taxes that go to the public schools. If you do the math the average student enrolled in elementary to secondary school will have $60,000 to $200,000 in tax dollars poured into the school they attend over their twelve years of compulsory attendance. Though this huge amount of money exists for every student who enrolls at a public institution, those who choose not to enroll their children receive zero financial aid, until they can apply for it for college and post-secondary studies. Despite this lack of monetary aid home educated students can and do achieve high levels of academic success and many have matriculated to esteemed and highly selective colleges, like Harvard, Stanford, Cornell, Princeton and others.

Recently an entire school district in Atlanta came under federal investigation for fraudulent test answers. Teachers in the district could earn a $20,000 bonus by producing higher test scores. You can imagine how such an incentive easily led to many teachers cheating. Along with the corruption in public schools, many families believe in leaving all the educating to the "educators." Few accept responsibility or actively involve themselves in what children are learning. Parents passively permit those who deem themselves professionals, who call themselves "certified teachers," to establish sole control over what children learn. Such an apathetic approach perpetuates a cycle of inactivity, laziness and failure. Children are not challenging themselves and/or parents do not challenge their children. Each child could potentially achieve amazing accomplishments. No one told Einstein what he could study and when. Some of the greatest minds in history benefited from home education. So the question remains: what sort of person are you? Do you expect things to be easy? Do you enjoy not dealing with your children during the day? Do you think children learn better while in a structured classroom? How do you relate to your children? Can you talk to them? Do you know anything about them, or do you expect teachers to carry the instructional burden with your children?

Not every teacher will support or pay attention to every child and not every student will ask for what he or she needs. When a student feels stupid, perceives him or herself as a failure, asking for help only increases those feelings of inferiority. If you're the only student raising your hand in class for help, then you must be a dummy. I know from my part-time job, leading a team of 8-10 college degreed adults, that only those more concerned with doing well, who don't worry about looking stupid, will ask questions. If asking questions results in other students judging you, or only confusing you more, then you won't ask until you feel confident enough to know it's alright to make mistakes. Otherwise you might feel stupid, asking for help when everyone else around you appears to understand. In truth, even a smart child struggles to understand the poorly written, often confusing, and frequently outdated information they must cover for homework and on exams. Not every child will understand the one-size-fits-all, cookie cutter curriculum created by their public school. Though each goes through the same molding process, they won't necessarily think the way the public schools assume they will. Force feed every student identical materials and each one will learn; at least that's what public schools dictate. Schools frequently function like an automated factory. If one little imperfection emerges in a product going down the production line, workers toss it. Apply this to schools and flawed students either drop-out or fail, further feeding low self-esteem.

Originated during the industrial age, public schools closely resemble the production lines that greatly benefited from an increase in marginally trained young people. Students could easily transition from the daily school schedule, designed to follow the same work schedule as factories, which included specific tasks to be finished in a set amount of time, eating lunch quickly and then returning to work when the whistle blows, I mean, when the bell rings. Schools mirror the same general structure as factories. Only recently do new school buildings include more contemporary options, more windows, beautiful spaces, and recreational activities. Older schools lack all of these innovations. You can put a silk dress on a pig and call it Sally, but it's still a pig. Schools might try to improve their appearances, but doing so doesn't really address the issues. Great disparities in education still remain. Some students attend shiny new school buildings which might include large indoor pools, wide open spaces, innovative common areas, and designer manicured green spaces. Yet others spend five days a week in stuffy buildings, with broken air conditioning units, leaking ceilings, libraries with few books, classrooms lacking supplies, playgrounds that consist of a dirt or blacktop yard, and no facilities for sports, music, or art. Children in those schools might rate a museum visit once a year, riding a bus two hours from a rural district, only to rush through an exhibit hall last updated in the 1980's.

I am not by any means implying that home education will solve every possible problem that a child will and can face, or that every family situation will provide a better learning environment. Reviewing the U.S. Census Bureau data on home education, the highest percentage of home educating families are Caucasian, and one parent works full time while the other either works just part time or stays at home. The decision to choose home education demands sacrifice and compromise. Hopefully this book offers some insight into home education and dispels some of the fallacies that permeate the media, so that some families might realize a possible alternative for something better for their children.

I hope this chapter portrays a more honest picture of the public education system. I sincerely hope beyond hope that all children end up in nurturing, positive public schools, exceptions to all the rules, schools in which they can flourish and achieve success, free of worry, peer pressure and bullying. Surely these schools exist, possibly, somewhere. I've met teachers who sincerely and deeply care about the success of their students, those who assist students way beyond the call of duty. However, due to the rarity of such teachers and schools, I hope that you will find the information and resources you need to become a successful home educating parent or home educated student after reading this book.

# So What About College?

*"In my opinion the prevailing systems of education are all wrong, from the first stage to the last stage. Education begins where it should terminate, and youth, instead of being led to the development of their faculties by the use of their senses, are made to acquire a great quantity of words, expressing the ideas of other men instead of comprehending their own faculties, or becoming acquainted with the words they are taught or the ideas the words should convey."-William Duane*

Whether or not someone attends college hinges on personal choice. Home educated and unschooled students must face this choice, just like their institutionally educated peers. Most colleges and universities now welcome home educated students. Getting admitted to college as an unschooled or home educated student follows the exact same steps and procedures as those coming out of structured school systems. One must usually complete the necessary exams, either the ACT or SAT, or both. Unschooled and home educated students can easily register for these exams and access study resources for these exams with online information from the College Board web site. For both home schoolers and their public school counterparts, this information is readily available to anyone considering applying to the majority of colleges and universities in the United States. Test centers do not discriminate against the unschooled student.

Unschooled students can study for both exams with online prep courses, preparatory books on loan from the library, by purchasing prep books from local bookstores, and with practice exams from a wide variety of sources, many of which are online and free.  Several websites offer both free study guides and practice tests, as well as those that students can purchase.  Most public libraries and bookstores stock their shelves with up to date versions of the latest ACT and SAT official preparatory books.  But I advise that students plan well ahead, since these books may fly off the shelves in the months before official test dates in October through May each year.

In this chapter I'd like to discuss how easily almost any unschooled student can enroll in college and the many options beyond sitting in college classrooms through which an unschooled student can earn college credit whenever ready.  I hope this chapter will quell the fears of many who suspect that an unschooled student can't easily gain college admission, or succeed in college after up to twelve years of unschooling.  To explain this I will relate my personal story about my experiences selecting and attending college.  Between the ages of 10 through 19 I pursued many passions.  My interests varied so dramatically from week to week that I can't imagine how my mother managed to keep her sanity.  Some days I spent hours practicing as a dedicated competitive figure skater and some days I didn't even want to put on my skates.  Around the age of 16, when dating distracted me, thoughts about my future fell to the wayside. I've witnessed this with many teenage girls.  Luckily my family and friends redirected my focus toward academics.

While a teen I worked at the public library, saved money for a car, and spent time with friends on weekends.  I really hadn't clearly pictured my future or considered what interested me. I've always felt jealous of those people who knew from a young age exactly where they intended to go to college and exactly what they would study.  If only I knew; if only I could think of just one possible road to travel. In the end I followed the one road that all my friends traveled, applying for college.  My mother encouraged me to attend college so I could realize my full potential by setting a clear goal, a four-year college degree, and completing it.  She also understood that spending time around my peers in an educational environment could prove that not attending school hadn't hurt me, from either a social or academic standpoint.

I harbored a secret, though, fearing that if I returned to public school that the school would place me in a lower grade because I wouldn't score high enough on their placement tests. Yes, that's right, I felt completely and totally insecure about my own education as an unschooler. Home educated students can't compare themselves to other students. Since most home educated students don't regularly take tests, they can't compare their test scores to those of publicly educated students, or any other students for that matter. I feared that I wasn't learning enough or working hard enough. I'm a perfectionist and I worried that unschooling might hold me back, might prevent me from excelling in college and later, in life. Though my mother reassured me over and over, and my ACT scores reflected that I wasn't any less intelligent than my friends, I still stressed about failing my college courses. Perhaps this fear kept me from applying to college until age 18, and then not attending until 19. I struggled with the guilt of not studying more regularly as an unschooler. I often criticized myself for watching too much television, spending too much time talking to friends and not enough time focusing on academic goals. Of course my mother never voiced her concern because she knew better.

After taking both the ACT and SAT, I discovered that, though I excelled in writing, reading, and science, I didn't score as well on math. Determined to avoid remedial math courses in college, I studied high school math, algebra through trigonometry, for about two months, right before my scheduled college entrance and placement exam. I finished the exam in ten minutes and learned that I had scored way above the remedial level. Stressing over not spending my last 8 years of education stuck in a classroom and studying math textbooks, doing pages and pages of homework problems, proved a waste of time, as my mother always told me. I realized that an unschooled student could dedicate a great deal less

142

time per day to studying and could learn and retain whatever colleges required to get accepted without remediation. For math in particular, as many as 75% of entering college freshmen must enroll in remedial courses during their first year of college.

When I started college in the fall of 2006 I didn't sleep before my first day of classes. Instead I tossed and turned, panicking, stressed, excited and overwhelmed all at once. Why? Because I hadn't stepped foot in an academic classroom environment for the better part of nine years and I believed that I didn't know what to expect. Would I find my classes? Would people notice anything different about me? Am I as smart as the other students? I often asked myself that last question. At the end of my first week of classes I knew the answer. I had arrived just as prepared for college as everyone else. I scored very well on all my papers. I passed my tests and I could actively, even vigorously, participate in classroom discussions.

When I graduated from college in the spring of 2010 I had earned a B.A. with a focus in Art. I was proud that even though I didn't go to public school, I had attended college and graduated in only four years. By writing this book I hope others will learn that any unschooled and home educated student who decides to attend college can fulfill all the necessary requirements and graduate in four years or less for most degree programs. While completing my undergraduate degree I maintained better than a "B" average. In my freshman year my grade point average of 3.87 earned me the Academic Excellence in Art, Humanities and Fine Arts Award.

My accomplishments pale in comparison to some other home educated students who have received amazing honors, awards and recognition for their academic achievements. I'm sure you've read news stories about home educated students who win spelling bees, or chess matches, or even the MacArthur Genius Award, but you seldom hear about how they achieved success on the collegiate and professional level. Immediately after graduation from college I began a job that required my four-year college degree. And after working for one year I earned a promotion to a supervisory position at my workplace. Earning a college degree qualified me for my job and opened the door for me to participate in an enjoyable and professional work environment.

I easily transitioned from unschooling to attending college classes and I enjoyed attending lectures and participating in class discussions. During my first few weeks in college I noticed my peers rarely attended lecture classes, except on exam days. Since I hadn't spent all those years sitting in classrooms, I wasn't bored or jaded in the lecture halls and was still open to learning from my professors. It appeared, however, that my peers had lost all interest. For example, in my sophomore course, Microbiology of Diseases, only a handful of students bothered showing up for the late afternoon lectures three times a week. Required to seek approval from an academic adviser in my major before I could enroll in each semester's courses, I set up an appointment with this adviser. His job was to insure that I fulfilled my required core courses in my major, fine arts, and he suggested that I not enroll in the microbiology course, but instead recommended a course that was fondly referred to as "rocks for jocks."

By my third week of classes the lecture halls, which could hold around 150 students, looked more like a small study group with only a dozen or fewer students. I figured other students simply dropped the course out of disinterest. However, on the first exam day (the first of four) the lecture hall quickly filled with students in nearly every seat. This lecture skipping pattern repeated in every lecture course I took. On every exam day the lecture halls grew crowded with unfamiliar faces. Yet, there I was, the unschooled student, who had never spent much time in a classroom, regularly attending all my classes. Completely confused by this phenomenon of students only showing up for exams, I soon learned that missing an exam meant failing the class, but if a student skipped every lecture he or she could still eek out a passing grade simply by taking all the exams. I wondered why my peers easily accepted this level of mediocrity, accepting near failing grades because they had missed out on the lectures. One of my friends cleared up my confusion with a short statement: "Once you graduate from college no one looks at your GPA, so it doesn't matter whether you have a "C" average or an "A" average. So basically all my peers who attended regular school at public and private institutions, who took the same ACT and SAT exams, and who were paying, or whose families were paying for their education, cared less about their academic success than I. Despite not receiving a single graded assignment in nine years of unschooling, I cared a great deal about the grades I received in college. When your parent is your only official teacher, you know firsthand the effort required to put together learning materials. You realize just how much effort the instructors put into their lectures and exams. Granted, some are better than others at this, but still, I could sense how disillusioned about teaching my professors felt when noticing that 50-80% of the students would only show up on exam days.

Unschooling taught me to love enriching my life through all kinds of learning and that love accompanied me to college where I elected many courses that interested me. Even though I followed the requirements of my degree program, I still discovered plenty of courses on subjects that simply attracted my interest. I couldn't understand why my supposedly better educated and better prepared peers, those who had attended schools and followed a curriculum, always stuck with courses in which they held little to no interest. Most home educated students search for new learning opportunities and proactively play a role in their own education. This can translate to the home educated and unschooled student excelling while in college. An unschooled student, armed with self-motivation and a proactive attitude, will seek out challenges, a characteristic of college students who excel both in college and later in their chosen life work. Without these self-directed qualities a student will, more often than not, fulfill only minimal required courses. While never technically held accountable for his or her own education, since no teachers or exam dates dictate when an unschooled student must show up or turn in specific assignments, you might assume that the unschooled student would turn out lazy and the least likely to qualify as a responsible and successful college student. Let me tell you from my own experience that failing oneself would be the greatest possible disappointment. If I had not completed my college degree, and finished it in a reasonable four-year time frame, I would have disappointed myself more than anyone else, and that's what mattered most to me.

Though no one measures self-directed academic success against specific guidelines and rubrics during compulsory attendance years, the unschooled student more often than not will measure him or herself against his or her own highest ideals, goals and aspirations. Since unschooled students don't follow timetables, a fixed curriculum, or standard subjects, some may begin to fulfill college curriculum, earning college credit, as early as 14 or 15 years of age. (Keep reading and I'll explain how anyone can start earning college credit, even in their early teens.) If a home educated student so elects, he or she can study for and complete College Level Examination Program (CLEP) courses for college credit during their high school years, with some who begin completing these college courses as early as age 14. Due to this relatively easy self-directed option they prepare themselves for college better than many other students and some will even graduate early. I've been told by many families that their children transitioned easily to college life and they reported that faculty, roommates and friends of home educated students never wondered about their educational background. For me the majority of my professors had no idea that I was home schooled, let alone unschooled, and they never asked me about my pre-college schooling.

Of course, I did encounter one instructor who accused me of plagiarism on my very first college paper in her English composition class because, she insisted, no home educated student could ever write such an outstanding paper. I proved her wrong, earning an "A" on every subsequent paper, though she never apologized, never retracted her humiliating accusation made in front of the whole class. From that experience I learned to never mention home education again, so that faculty prejudices couldn't interfere with my grades.

Not only do home educated students succeed and positively impact their college classrooms, perhaps due to a strong sense of moral conviction and outstanding family support, more often than not they will enroll in challenging courses, enjoying the opportunity to study advanced mathematics and science. Unlike many of their publicly educated peers, home educated students often enjoy greater access to Internet resources at home, frequent trips to museums, volunteer activities, and early work experiences. Home educated and unschooled students can concentrate on specific subjects for unlimited time periods, especially those topics that interest them, thus developing academic abilities and excelling at a much faster rate than many publicly schooled peers.

Of course, everyone knows that college presents plenty of opportunities to party, get drunk, indulge in drugs, and to behave in otherwise undesirable ways. Unschooled students often enjoy a strong and supportive family who encourage not just responsibility for educational goals, but also for personal behavior. Really, these two go hand in hand. If students grow up fully responsible for what they learn and how they learn, they usually hold themselves accountable for whether they will fail or succeed in life. These students realize that this sense of personal responsibility carries through everything they might decide to accomplish, not just graduating from college.

For the unschooled student college represents the cumulative sum of years spent as a self-motivated individual. College fulfills an unschooled student's possible need for self-affirmation from someone other than their parents and provides the student insight into how much they did or did not learn. I noticed that very few fellow students showed up for lectures, or spent any time studying. My college peers joked about how attending classes prevented them from enjoying college, or rather from attending parties. Going to classes and studying, they bemoaned, felt like a form of punishment and not an opportunity to gain knowledge. I couldn't relate to their misery. I attended my classes and I studied. Whenever possible I arrived early and reviewed my notes. When I graduated from college I demonstrated that a totally nontraditional education can indeed provide a solid foundation for higher education.

Unschooled students may enjoy attending free lectures offered at some universities and colleges. For most unschooled students learning experiences in the community could open doors and improve social skills. Education represents an experience, not a chore, and not something unhappily endured by students. Most unschooled students embrace and enjoy a wide variety of learning opportunities.

So the unschooler can go to college. Or let's say, he or she will go to college and will graduate. Ignore what those other people say if they suggest anything different. If they still won't listen, simply point to this book and say this unschooler did it. I decided to attend an academically challenging university. I wanted a degree from a prestigious school, so I attended a prestigious state-supported university. However, since my college path was one designed by necessity for a lower income student, I must admit that I spent my first year of college commuting to a satellite campus. There I found that the smaller classes meant that I had better show up for every session and not be one of the slackers who only shows up on exam days. After the first week in a class with only 10 to 20 students the profs learned every student's name and would pull aside those who failed to show up for classes, or who arrived late.

Since these satellite campus classes were small the profs really took the time to get to know their students on a personal level. They would talk to students before and after class. They would sit down with students and go over papers. Even though I had felt a little ashamed that I couldn't afford to attend the main campus with all its classiness and prestige, I discovered in the end that I had received a higher level of education from my instructors that first year while attending the satellite campus. There's nothing shameful about being one of ten students in a class and attending classes under professors who truly care about their students. They helped me realize the importance of seeking out the best possible education for myself. I hope that unschoolers won't ever limit themselves, thinking they could never attend college. Set this as a goal early, in seventh or eighth grade, if possible. Take it from me, someone whose family couldn't afford to pay for college, and from someone who had never seriously considered attending college, there is nothing more satisfying then saying: "I was unschooled and I graduated from college and have a full-fledged, fully accredited Bachelor of Arts degree."

### Preparing For College

For most unschooled students or the parents of an unschooled student, eventually thoughts of college arise. Preparing for college should begin as early as possible. Unschooled and home educated students can attend college as young as age 15, if they'd like, possibly even earlier depending on the policies of the college. Pre-teen and teen unschooling students, not emotionally prepared and lacking the maturity or interest to begin college in their early teens, can still earn credit toward a college degree in other ways.

Most colleges now accept applications from home educated students and home educated students receive the same sort of academic, athletic and federal aid as their publicly educated counterparts. Since no one has determined an exact number of just how many home educated students attend college, I can state from personal experience that out of the home schooling families I knew, most of the 18-19 year-olds did apply, were accepted, and attended at least some college. From what I noticed, those who attended college enjoyed popularity, appeared well-adjusted, did well in classes, and behaved just like other coeds.

College can carry high costs, both monetary and emotional. So thoroughly discuss both the pros and cons of the college experience. Consider looking first at colleges within affordable traveling distance for your family, so if your student wants to return home during breaks from class or over the summer, you won't pay for expensive transportation and storage costs. For me that type of travel cost more than my family could afford. So, I chose to look at colleges no more than two hours driving distance from my home. This is one of those times when living in a major metropolitan area really helped. Within two hours of my home I located numerous private and public colleges and universities, literally dozens.

Aside from traveling costs to and from the college, students and parents should consider tuition costs, as well as room and board costs. I probably could have mentioned this first, since all these costs usually determine if a student can attend a particular college. However, families often ignore some of the other costs that can financially overburden them. Some of my friends mistakenly attended a college on the opposite side of the country from their families, only to realize the challenges and costs of living that far away. So evaluate all the possible costs, do the math, considering not only tuition, but also travel expenses, supplies, books, furnishings, cloths, laundry, health insurance (required by most colleges), cell phone, computers, and incidentals. Also think about things like the fees for keeping a car on campus, if allowed.

Now that you've considered how college will financially impact you and your family, you should research what sorts of college programs will work best for you. Will a home educated or unschooled student need to attend classes on a college campus or would an online program work just as well, or perhaps better? Does a residential college strongly appeal to you or your student? Can the student maturely and responsibly handle living away from home? Students can earn a college degree in a number of ways, some of which won't require a full four years spent living in a college town. Whichever route you choose, make sure that you know the accreditation of the institution in which you enroll, that the school belongs to an accepted accreditation organization, that it maintains good retention and graduation rates. The last of these is of utmost importance, so carefully check out those graduation rates. Do students graduate in 4 years or less? Beware of four-year colleges where the majority of students graduate in five, six, or more years.

Colleges and universities in which students frequently take five to six years to finish a degree program may not offer enough sections of some classes required for degree completion. For example, they may only offer certain courses during certain semesters. If the student has filled his or her schedule, or the campus boasts a very active party scene that distracts students from their studies, he or she might not finish course work on time, which can also delay graduation. Trust me, if you are struggling to pay for four years of college, then you will cringe over the cost of five to six years worth of college debt. Keep in mind that federal aid only covers undergrads for the first four and sometimes five years of college. After that you must rely on loans from private lending institutions. I can't emphasize this enough, so pretend that I'm saying what follows super loudly and intensely: do not take out private loans, ever! If federal aid will not cover your costs, then find a more affordable school or program, get a job, but do not ever resort to private loans. These loans carry high interest rates and can hurt your credit rating for decades. Federal loans offer lower rates and a variety of options for repayment, along with the ability to

151

temporarily defer loans, if needed. Many impacted by a recession economy have benefitted from these loan deferments.

In my experience the institutions that hold my federal loans have been very helpful, readily granting a deferment while unemployed. I chose an affordable college program and I also worked while in college. I paid off anything left after my federal loans and grants came through. Finding the right college and adequate scholarships will absorb much of your time, so expect to research for weeks to months. Start selecting a college early. Below I've listed the resources I used to get accepted and to graduate from college in four years or less, while accruing a manageable amount of debt. Please check out these resources and information as guides to help you or your unschooled student reach the goal of college graduation.

## ACT

I preferred the ACT exam as the best assessment for the unschooling student. You may take the ACT multiple times, if necessary. Some public schools even offer first-time fee waivers for students, which includes homeschooled or unschooled students. Tax dollars support these fee waivers which apply to all students in a district. So check with your public school district's high school guidance counselor to find out if they offer waivers and how you can apply for one, if needed.

Studying for the ACT requires focus, focus, and more focus. Libraries loan preparation and practice exam books for free, or you can buy them at book stores, and you can find many additional resources online. Tutoring could help, but honestly, taking as many practice exams as possible works best. Complete each entire exam, then go over the results and focus on your weak points. Research those weak areas and keep practicing the four sections of the exam until you feel confident that you know all the subjects well. Don't worry, you can repeat the exam again if you don't do well the first time. Just allow enough time (months to years) for the required waiting period before students can repeat this exam.

Registering for the ACT is easy. When you show up for the exam, don't forget to take a legal photo I.D. Once in the exam room you have two hours to complete the first part with one brief break, and then you may take up to two more hours to complete the full exam. Those four hours will pass quickly. As an unschooler you shouldn't fear taking this exam, even if this is your first exam experience. You simply bubble in your responses with your number two pencil. After you receive your exam results you can research the colleges to which you'd like to apply, and discover if your scores will qualify you for admission into those particular institutions. If not, don't worry; try another institution, or retake the exam and raise your scores.

If you try the ACT in your early teens you will more clearly understand where you should focus. Consider this a gift. Now you know where you stand, more or less, with your peers who attend traditional schools. I remember how satisfied I felt when I discovered that I had scored one point above a friend of mine who often bragged about her elitist high school. It pleased me because I didn't sit through hours and hours of classes or take lots of exams like she did, yet I scored just as well on the ACT.

## www.collegeresults.org

If only I had found this website when I was 18 and first applying for college, but now I can recommend it as a guide for deciding both undergrad and graduate school possibilities. This website allows you to search by college and find out important statistics, such as acceptance rates, actual attendance rates, tuition costs, faculty to student ratios, etc. Students and parents will find a wealth of information on this website and can quickly evaluate what each college offers. Want to attend a more diverse campus? Or do you want to learn the median ACT and SAT score requirements for the school? You can do so very easily on this website without digging through often confusing college or university websites. In addition you can quickly search and get a snapshot insight into multiple colleges.

**www.myfuture.com**

Know you want to go to college, but unsure about what to study? At this website you can search by degree programs. Interested in studying anthropology? Then you can search by interest and find out the average income and the education level of those already working in that field. It also explains, for example, that about 63% of those working in anthropology must have earned a doctoral degree. You can also discover if that field is increasing or decreasing in job demand. Through this website you can determine the best higher education program and the required degree level you would need for success in that field.

**CLEP**

When I started my senior year of college I was six credits short for graduation. Since I knew about CLEP (College Level Examination Program) I contacted my college program director and asked about earning those six credits toward my degree by taking two CLEP exams, one for psychology and another for sociology. My program director and I reviewed my college transcripts and agreed upon these two CLEP exams to fulfill my degree requirements. I was thrilled because the two CLEP exams cost a little less than $200 total for the six credits I needed. Otherwise I could have enrolled in six extra credits, in addition to my standard 15 credits per semester, which would have cost me an additional $400 per credit hour, or $2400 more for that semester. That savings really helped, especially near the end of my senior year. I studied between semesters for these exams and didn't overburden myself while completing my other course work.

The organization that handles these exams is the College Board, the same organization behind the SAT and AP. CLEP exams represent what you would cover on a final exam for a college course. Each exam lasts no longer than 90 minutes and all but one, College Composition, is multiple choice. The number of questions on each exam varies from 90-140, depending on the subject. CLEP exams cost $80 which you pay to the College Board and also pay a small fee to the college testing service wherever they take the exam. Students pay these fees at the time they take the exam, not months before, like the SAT, ACT or AP exams, or even regular college courses. You will write two separate checks, one to the school administering the test and one to College Board. Did I mention that $80 is for three to six college credit hours for each course? Compare that to what you would pay at a college per credit hour, not including all the other fees associated with college courses.

CLEP exams offer an amazing resource for an unschooled or home schooled student, who can take any CLEP exam when he or she has a valid photo I.D. and when the student feels adequately prepared for the test. Best of all, the testing center usually administers these exams on a computer in a private and quiet area reserved for testing, where you will view your score on the monitor instantly upon completion of the exam. With no waiting or stressing about whether you pass or fail the test, you will get a paper copy validating your score before your leave the testing center. Also, if you're already enrolled in college the testing center can send the score directly to your college or university for free. If not currently enrolled CLEP maintains the scores on file for twenty years, so a student can order copies sent to the college of their choice at a later date. On the College Board website you can find out more information about how to register and search for colleges in your area that offer these exams, as well as colleges that accept CLEP credits toward a degree program. Taking these exams students can earn college credit while determining college preparedness in a particular subject. They can also familiarize themselves with college level exams, and further their college degree goals in an affordable and highly convenient way.

To study for CLEP exams look no further than your local library, your neighborhood bookstores, or the Internet. Public libraries usually loan back editions of CLEP study guide books, and students can purchase the newest preparation guides at most book stores. Also search the Internet for tons of free study resources. Just think, students can select a subject that interests them, study and prepare for it using many available study resources. Then students can schedule an exam at their convenience, paying for it at the time of the exam, and potentially can earn credit toward their college degree for less than $100 for three to six college semester credit hours. How much better can it get?

To receive credit one must score at or above the ACE (The American Council on Eduction) recommended score. CLEP exams don't rely on letter grades, but instead a scaled score of 20-80. At the following website you can learn more about taking CLEP exams: http://clep.collegeboard.org/
I highly recommend the addition of CLEP exams to any unschooling student's high school equivalent years, especially if that student might pursue a college degree.

Currently students may choose from 33 different CLEP exams. However, a college may decide whether to accept CLEP credits toward a degree program, or not, and may only accept credits for certain exams. Check with each college that the unschooling student is considering attending and choose exams the colleges do accept and that will fulfill required foundation or survey courses at that institution. Whether preparing for the SAT, ACT or CLEP exams, students can easily create a study plan and follow it for weeks or months. Should a student fail to earn the required score that would qualify for credit on a CLEP exam, any student may repeat the exam, but must wait six months. So don't take the exam until your practice tests clearly indicate that you have fully prepared.

I earned my six credits toward my degree and that fulfilled two core fundamentals required at my university. To graduate on time, I could only spend about two to three weeks cramming for both the Introduction to Psychology exam in the fall, and then the Introduction to Sociology exam between semesters in the winter. Luckily I passed both the first time I tried to take them. CLEP exams saved me both time and money.

# The Lifelong Learner

*"Since we can't know what knowledge will be most needed in the future, it is senseless to try to teach it in advance. Instead, we should try to turn out people who love learning so much and learn so well that they will be able to learn whatever needs to be learned."- John Holt*

I've written about how the unschooled student can go to college and succeed and I mentioned some of the many great accomplishments home educated students have achieved. I've told you about my personal experiences, some anecdotes, and shared my knowledge. Since I am only in my twenties as I write this, I recognize that my knowledge is limited, but I do deserve some credit. Even though this book not only showed how you can quit school, teach yourself, and go to college, it also revealed a great deal about my life, which I hope expresses just how deeply I care for and believe in unschooling. Actually, more than just unschooling, I deeply care for and believe in the potential of America's young people. I don't want to see some of America's best and brightest youth so discouraged and disillusioned by this often superficial and fickle society that they forgo fulfilling their own educational goals and dreams.

Recently I've thought a great deal about my aspirations, my own goals and dreams. I set out to write this book over two years ago. However, despite my strong opinions on many things and my passion for a number of topics, I have yet to truly feel confident about my role as a writer. Realizing that my own anxiety limits my ability, I figure it probably limits the ability of many young people to follow their dreams. In a traditional school environment, where everyone faces so much drama, stress, pressure, disillusionment, and where many struggle for identity, sometimes personal dreams or aspirations can appear way beyond one's reach.

While students are attending and completing college degree requirements many will realize what they aspire to achieve someday, and others will discover these preferences earlier, perhaps through school athletics and other personal experiences and influences. Many who stand outside the homeschooling community don't perceive that the home educated student can achieve success or complete personal goals, due to a lack of structure, focus, or direction. In my experience this is most definitely not the case. Even though many home educated students waffle about what they'd like to do when they "grow up," are just as indecisive as their institutionally schooled peers, somehow home schoolers do manage to get on track. The majority of home educated students I've known follow through and pursue an academically oriented path, completing college and graduate school to become artists, biologists, writers, and professionals in many fields.

Any parent would proudly celebrate if their child wrote a successful book, graduated from veterinary or medical school, or entered the world of classical music as an orchestra member or composer. Not every home educated or unschooled student will aspire to do amazing things, but without the limiting constructs of institutionalized learning many unschooled students strive to fulfill an endless array of dreams and personal aspirations. Some might study history and discover links to the future through understanding the past. Some might find the complexities and nuances found in calculus or physics truly intrigue them, seeking a career in the mathematical or scientific fields.

Since my own alternative education led me to explore a multitude of possible career paths, I never perceived that working a typical 9-5 job was my only option. No one ever told me that I couldn't attempt interesting and more challenging goals, if I wanted to pursue them. Well, okay, a few well-intentioned people did try to dissuade me, but I ignored them. So far my life as an unschooler has revolved around pursuing a variety of difficult goals. In the beginning I dreamed of being an amazing figure skater, setting goals to earn gold medals and to skate in ice shows. Though I won my share of gold medals, I, like so many other young people, discovered many new interests that pulled me in other directions.

When I chose to follow an unschooling path I discovered amazing opportunities, often electing to embrace some of the less certain, but enthralling chances and experiences that life offers. While I knocked on doors to follow my dreams, other children, caught in the social drama and regimen of the usual years in public school, often struggle to hear the voice in their heads that leads them to dream about what they could achieve.

Thus few dare to dream and even fewer take the necessary risks. My years of unschooling taught me that risks are part of life, and, yes, rejection and disappointment, too. Those stuck in public school might fear peer rejection and that could prevent them from ever considering anything more than whatever their friends discuss, or whatever their popular culture spoon-feeds them. Often it appears that television and online video viewing so thoroughly fill the minds of many young people that all personal thought disappears in a babble of celebrity gossip, social networking status updates and tweets.

Once people dreamed, sought to innovate, create, and inspire their generation and their country. Today writers, artists, philosophers and inventors rarely get much support and thus very few fulfill their dreams. When I see a home educated or unschooled child I perceive a future uninhibited by instructional limitations and filled with great potential. I hope for them and dream for them. I want them to succeed in ways that I've never even considered because I so strongly believe in the alternative educational option of unschooling. Perhaps I'm only basing this on my own personal experience, but from what I've observed firsthand our educational systems fail to increase or foster the inherent intelligence of all students, let alone to encourage creativity or innovation, both of which form the backbone of a functioning and developing society.

If you don't believe me then study art history where you can learn that some of the greatest artistic minds designed buildings so beautiful and of such extraordinary structure and quality that most are still standing today. Look to Rome whose epic buildings still stand as icons of a society that nurtured its creative and innovative citizens. Will you and your children recognize those buildings? Will you know the names of the dreamers behind them? What if you or your child understood that a single person could design and create something of such reverence and strength that centuries later it still stands as a reminder of humanity's ingenuity? Would that knowledge change you or your child for the better? An unschooled student can elect to study such places and people, can focus on artists like Michelangelo or Leonardo da Vinci, and they could sketch and design the buildings of the future without setting foot in anything that resembles the institutional schools of today.

Often people associate dreamers with liberal, foolish, and overly idealistic people. Mention that you dream of doing something and many people will roll their eyes at you, unless you dream of doing something practical, like becoming a nurse or a teacher. But if you want to change the world with art? Well, I'm sure you can imagine how some people just nod and silently judge such unrealistic aspirations. Unschooling represents this kind of dream. Just try explaining it to your family and they will most likely call you misguided, impractical, even irresponsible.

Though most dreamers face discouragement, as I know firsthand, don't allow yourself to be discouraged and don't submit your child to the daily discouragement of schools. In schools criticism and judgment can run rampant and can control students like an addictive drug. Those who want to do anything considered outside the norm will face the risk of getting bullied. Heck, those who make a mistake get bullied, and those who dress differently get bullied. Yes, I know that bullies exist everywhere and in every situation, but they should not thrive in the buildings where a child is required by law to attend five days a week, supposedly for learning. No effective learning curriculum should ever include teasing, taunting, and ridicule. Who you are and what you wear, how much money your family earns, your racial identity, sexual orientation, or personal beliefs should not interfere with your ability to learn.

Outside the classroom, beyond institutional walls, away from social anxieties, shallow relationships, peer pressures, and bullying, all of which dominate the average classroom environment, a great education awaits you. While many publicly educated students look back on their days in school as a form of punishment, unschooled students fondly remember how they acquired lifelong learning skills. Ask any student today whether they like going to school and the majority will say no. Given the choice most children would prefer to stay at home for a variety of reasons. Some fear bullies, others feel they aren't smart enough, attractive enough, or wealthy enough to have any friends. In the eyes of these children school doesn't equal the joy of learning; it equals a monotonous, unavoidable experience in which they only look forward to recess and lunch, and not what they will learn in the classroom between those breaks.

With our current system of education young people face boredom and often find education unsatisfactory, if not just plane useless. Teachers instructing from a book seldom incite a fervid desire to learn in every child. Those who respond better to more interactive or hands on approaches will find book learning frustrates them, limiting what they retain. In public schools when a student doesn't respond to the particular way a teacher presents learning material, that student will often flounder and fail.

Instilling in children that they should blame only themselves for their failure to learn breeds a hatred for authority figures and instruction, when children should never carry the burden of ineffective teaching practices. Allowing children to feel inferior everyday when they enter a classroom, convincing them of their weaknesses while the school avoids the blame for their failures, does not sound like a good system to me. And it shouldn't to you, either.

When children lose confidence in themselves and their ability to learn, problems simmer on the back burner, often coming to a boil when they reach adulthood. If you've ever felt incapable of achieving because that's what twelve years of institutionalized learning taught you, then you might not aim for much in your life. I've heard many stories from friends and family members about teachers and counselors inferring that college or more challenging academic courses would be too difficult for them. Even with excellent grades in college, my academic advisor during my sophomore year of college suggested I register for an easier geology course, instead of the microbiology course I wanted. Against the advice of my advisor, I chose to take both the regular geology course, as well as the microbiology course, receiving a "B" in both courses. Clearly, no one else can accurately judge the intellectual abilities of another, and in my specific case my college academic adviser underestimated my determination and perseverance. Public schools constantly underestimate student learning potential, relying on assessments that can't truly measure a child's abilities, and teachers who barely know the learning needs of their students. Misguided opinions of teachers should never determine how far a student might progress in life.

Home educated families want the best of everything possible for their children, defining success by the places they've gone, the projects they complete, the hours spent together exploring new ideas and discovering stimulating lessons in every day life. Parents should never accept that everyone must follow the specific dictates of their public school faculty and administration.

# The Unschooling Adult

Applying the same principles learned as an unschooling child to my adult life enhances both my job and my personal life. Unschooling freed me to approach problems from various viewpoints, so that I don't lock myself into one form of problem solving. In my work experience I have met some adults who struggle to perceive a problem from more than one possible angle. Often they will focus entirely, almost stubbornly, on a singular technique, one that worked for them while in school or college. For example, those from a very technical background might only elect to process information in front of them in a technical manner. Such rigidity can precipitate issues in a workplace, since employers prefer those who easily adjust and adapt to changing work situations. Flexibility literally defines unschooling. To unschool individuals and families must remain constantly open, prepared to readjust and reevaluate all aspects of the learning process. When issues arise an unschooler will, more often than not, automatically seek a creative solution, whether at home, at college or at work.

Unlike those "schooled" in a traditional setting, unschooled children understand the value of creative problem solving. If unschooled children want to participate in art programs, but their families can't afford these programs, they will search until they find a way to study art for little to no cost. If the unschooled child enjoys electronics, robots, or computers, he or she will discover ways to study how to work with and build them. The possible subjects and activities available to the unschooler are limited only by the student's imagination, creating an individual potentially adept at many fields of study. Staying pigeonholed in a single field of study, or on an institutional learning track that only elaborates on a very limited range of course content, does not expand the kinds of skill sets needed to gain an advantage in today's rapidly changing work environment. Unschooled adults, on the other hand, may bring unique skill sets to the workplace: great communication skills from conversing with a wider age group; independence and self-reliance from self-directed learning pursuits; creativity and focus from interest-based studies; and self-motivation to sustain efficient, goal oriented direction. The biggest asset that unschooled adults can offer is that they expect to further their personal knowledge and to expand on what they've learned throughout life. For the unschooler learning doesn't ever stop because education presents itself all the time. Suddenly every place, every situation, can create learning opportunities and experiences that hone acuity or aptitude for a wide range of activities.

After all that I have already written it probably won't surprise you to learn that unschoolers can mature into well-adjusted adults. Personal growth and acceptance develop naturally, along with responsibility for life choices and foresight to consider the consequences of those choices. Even parents benefit from the unschooling journey. I've heard from parents about how much they enjoy sharing in the activities in which their children participate and how that bonds their family together. Despite sacrifices, like not getting that eight-hour break each day when children attend school, these parents gratefully spend that time with their children instead. Without the support of my parents throughout my life and with me everyday, I might not have confidently pursued the immense task of writing this book. Instead I extended what I had learned from my unschooling childhood and decided to face yet another challenge, to wrestle with another lofty goal.

Knowing that my parents chose to keep me around all the time and to participate actively in my interests and in my life activities continues to motivate me and persistently inspires me to seek opportunities to better myself. I actively question how I might improve myself, in my life, in my job, and in my relationships. For me unschooling has never ended; instead it has simply extended into all other aspects of my life. I'm always expanding my knowledge on topics that interest me. Unschooling has instilled in me an appetite for information beyond what students usually study in a classroom or what workers learn on the job. Without my unorthodox "schooling," I doubt that I would strive nearly as hard as I do, or continue to set so many lofty personal goals and aspirations.

I've seen my publicly schooled peers grow up and get jobs. We spend time together nearly every weekend. Though my education appears diametrically opposed to theirs, I still connect and form friendships with those who attended schools. How one learns doesn't stop one from finding and cultivating friends, nor does it deter success later in life. Instead unschoolers can mature into well rounded adults, well equipped to attend college, qualify for jobs and form meaningful personal relationships. In the realm of unschooling learning neither sustains limitations nor hampers freedom of thought, like it can in public school. Individuals who "graduate" from unschooling often reflect on the importance of self-growth and independence. No one will tell you what to do, what to expect, or upon what page one will locate necessary life instructions. Instead every choice arises from one's personal desire, one's independent drive, instilling a passion for continued learning and building great strength of character. Deciding to improve oneself, to take on new challenges, to attend college, or to pursue some other goal, requires that strength.

Unschooling fosters a strong sense of self. In school the self can get lost in the fog of peer pressure, bullying, and wasted time. Children need to grow into self-reliant and self-motivated adults, individuals who realize that failure doesn't exist, only more ways to approach a challenge. Those who enjoy the process of learning also discover that they delight in either going to college or in a pursuing a career. Unschooling fosters independent thinkers who redefine the parameters of learning. Not confined to a rigidly structured and flawed system of education, unschooled adults realize the need to further expand their knowledge throughout life. Freed from twelve years of force-fed curriculum, curriculum that often fails to support necessary life skills, skills needed to solve many everyday problems, these adults may face many issues, such as the inability to succeed in college, or to progress in a work environment.

Institutionalized learning frequently forgets to encourage simple common sense thinking. Publicly schooled adults aren't taught how to manage money, how to handle bank accounts, loans, or credit cards. Read evidence of this on the government loan website that posts thousands of complaints from college students who didn't understand the terms of loan agreements and now are struggling to pay back mountains of debt. Ask them what they learned in school about how interest rates increase and loans ballon to unimaginably high amounts, or how school never taught them how to balance a checkbook, or how to build good credit. All this very basic knowledge about how to sustain oneself in a home, with a car, a job, and how to support a family does not appear in most standard school textbooks or curricula.

Instead the typical school curriculum focuses on those exams that measure academic progress, more commonly known as assessment exams, or tests that supposedly measure how knowledge increases from elementary school through high school. For the most part these tests simply indicate whether or not a student attended class and memorized information placed before them, and if the student can understand and follow simple directions, skills appropriate for most ordinary jobs. So, what sort of future do you want for your child? What sort of future do you foresee for yourself? Do you really believe that the public school system honestly offers the best educational opportunities?

## See the Forest for the Trees

As a child I loved all the trees that surrounded the house in which I grew up. I remember drawing those trees over and over again, using every shade of green crayon I could find, until the branches held leaves of every possible hue. For my thesis in my senior year of college, I wrote about all the greens of my trees, explaining how each tree and every individual leaf differed so greatly, especially if, as an artist, one spent the time to truly look closely. Every branch told a different story and every leaf a different piece of that story. Some branches were gnarled, some broken, some full of holes, and others perfect sweeping curves cascading to the ground in finger-thin tendrils. Some leaves would fall away, harboring scars, mars and hitchhikers.

Every tree told a story: recalling tales of a terrible storm, a bird's life, a bug infestation, a previous use as part of a fence or dog run. I imagined all the things each tree had survived. I wondered about how something that could appear so fragile could yet stand so tall against the fierceness of our mountain winters and seasonal hail storms, or glistening coats of heavy ice. I've seen how some trees, unable to bear the weight of their heavily ice and snow burdened limbs, will snap and fall to the ground with destructive grace. I've seen other trees bent and destroyed by the sheer forceful pounding of unforgiving winds.

I realized that the qualities I admired in trees were qualities I sought to acquire for myself. I wanted to grow up into a person who could stand tall, a strong person, someone who could withstand any storm. I wanted to always realize both the fragility and strength of life. I wanted to search for the beauty and complexities, the stories that people bury deep within themselves, like the stories written and revealed to scientists on the rings within a tree.

You might wonder why I'm writing about trees in this book about unschooling. Each person hides a story within them, something below the surface, or left behind in a scar, a wry smile, a distinctive laugh. People tend to view trees as part of a forest or woods, not as separate or unique forms. I suspect that many people like to look at children the same way. In a school children blend into the forest of other children, not seen as individuals, with no stories to tell other than what one perceives from a distance, through a quick wide-angle snapshot. Unschooling looks at the individual beauty in each and every child, much the way I considered the beauty of every single tree.

Through unschooling the strength and imagination of each child shines, stands out like a tree on a hilltop. Used often for inspiration and classic metaphoric symbolism, the image of a single tree, like the tree of life, proudly standing alone with branches laden with fruit or colorful leaves, reminds me of individual beauty, imagination, perseverance and potential. Nurtured by the environment, each child is like seed, growing as he or she absorbs the nutrients of life, everything in life's classrooms that surround the child, particularly during compulsory schooling years. In the woods the trees all appear uniform so that one could easily miss the subtle differences, the shapes of the leaves, the patterns of the bark. I think that in school children can too easily get lost in the woods and aren't seen as distinct beings. Whatever differences imbue each child with grace, strength, intelligence and uniqueness can hide unnoticed in a system that only focuses on test results, on the strengths of many, and not the strengths, needs and aspirations of each individual. You can't truly appreciate or understand any individual's complete nature until you see that individual for exactly what he or she is, a single human being, completely one-of-kind, who, just like a tree, is reaching upward, aiming toward the sky.

# References

Bauman, Kurt J.. "Home Schooling in the United States: Trends and Characteristics." . U.S Census Bureau, September 13, 2001. Web. 30 Sep 2012. <http://www.census.gov/population/www/documentation/twps0053/twps0053.html>.

"Bully Facts & Statistics." MBNBD. Make Beats Not Beat Downs. Web. 17 Oct 2012. <http://www.makebeatsnotbeatdowns.org/facts_new.html>.

Chan, Sewell. "The Highest Per-Pupil Spending in the U.S.." . The New York Times, May 24, 2007. Web. 30 Sep 2012. <http://empirezone.blogs.nytimes.com/2007/05/24/the-highest-per-pupil-spending-in-the-us/>.

"CDC- Suicide Prevention." Centers for Disease Control and Prevention. Centers for Disease Control and Prevention. Web. 17 Oct 2012. <http://www.cdc.gov/ViolencePrevention/suicide/index.html>.

Katz , Neil. "Schools Battle Suicide Surge, Anti-Gay Bullying." . CBS News, October 11, 2010. Web. 30 Sep 2012. <http://www.cbsnews.com/8301-504763_162-20019163-10391704.html>.

Leonard, Brooke. "Suicide rate increases in teens as an effect of bullying." Collegiate Times. Collegiate Times, April, 27, 2010. Web. 30 Sep 2012. <http://www.collegiatetimes.com/stories/15450/suicide-rate-increases-in-teens-as-an-effect-of-bullying>.

Pant, Meagan. "Ohio universities won't offer remedial classes." . Springfield News-Sun, 17 2012. Web. 17 Oct 2012. <http://www.springfieldnewssun.com/news/news/ohio-universities-wont-offer-remedial-classes-1/nPgcQ/>.

"Public Elementary–Secondary Education Finance Data." . United States Census Bureau, June 21, 2012. Web. 30 Sep 2012. <http://www.census.gov/govs/school/>

Sung-Jun, Chung. "In ranking, U.S. students trail global leaders." . USA Today, December 7, 2010. Web. 30 Sep 2012. <http://usatoday30.usatoday.com/news/education/2010-12-07-us-students-international-ranking_N.htm>.

"Teen Health." Preventing Teen Suicide. WebMD, February 03, 2012. Web. 30 Sep 2012. <http://teens.webmd.com/preventing-teen-suicide>.

"Teenage suicide in the United States." . Wikipedia, September 22, 2012. Web. 30 Sep 2012. <http://en.wikipedia.org/wiki/Teenage_suicide_in_the_United_States>.

"Teen Health." Preventing Teen Suicide. WebMD, February 03, 2012. Web. 30 Sep 2012. <http://teens.webmd.com/preventing-teen-suicide>.